TOSS

A New Offensive Attack for High-Scoring Football

JERRY VALLOTTON

The Toss

Edition revised 2009

By Jerry Vallotton

Copyright 1997 by Jerry Vallotton

All rights reserved. Charts and diagrams in this book may be reproduced by individual coaches for their teams. Reproduction of these materials for an entire school system is strictly forbidden.

Published by Accent Digital Publishing

Redding, CA

www.accentdigitalpublishing.com

ISBN   978-1-60445-042-8

The After-Chapter

If you are reading this then you are a football coach (current or former) interested in the doublewing offense. My first edition was published in 1997 in hardback. Since then I have had the privilege of corresponding with hundreds of great coaches all over the nation with a passion for coaching. I am happy to assist anyone willing to do the hard work of coaching football. I believe very few people have more impact on a young man's life than his football coach.

When I wrote "The Toss," the doublewing was still primarily on the west coast and still a very small cult of crazy coaches who were in some way influenced by its designer – Don Markham. Since then, through word of mouth and the explosion of the internet and all its components, this attack has spread like wildfire and can be seen as a prominent part of every state's football culture. However, it is still relatively unique enough that if you choose to run it you will most likely be the only one in your league, or area, who does.

The challenge now is to become a master technician of the doublewing. The "smash mouth" overload concept is still the essential element of the heart of this attack, but like all new offenses, over time defenses begin to catch up. What is fascinating about this one is that mere knowledge of how it works does not necessarily help a defensive coach stop it. But, over time good coaches teach, drill, and mold technique in order to have a fighting chance versus the onslaught of bodies coming at them. It is your job as a dedicated coach to "out-teach" and "out-refine" your opponents. You will not win championships simply because you have discovered a great new attack. This is why I am encouraging coaches to re-read "The Toss" and remember why and how it worked from the beginning. I think this makes for a great launching point.

Looking back over the past 20 years, it is great to see how this so-called "fad" or "gimmick" offense has stood the test of time. It is also great to see young coaches with fresh visions make it their own and tweak it – at the heart of the doublewing offense there still beats the desire to thoroughly dominate a defense using the team concept of 11 men. Plus the fact that year in and year out it can be effective regardless of personnel (which is crucial to a coach who cannot go shopping for players each year.)

In my humble opinion (after observing hundreds of examples) – Don Markham is still a genius and there is no greater thrill than running over a defense using the "smash mouth" concepts within the doublewing attack.

Best wishes,
Jerry Vallotton

Acknowledgements

In researching and writing this book, I had the help of many friends and colleagues. These are a few people who advised, supported, and assisted me: Kevin Askeland, Phil Bravo, Roland Banderob, Him Boesiger, Bryon Hamilton, Eric Hamzy, Don Markham, Herman Masin, Dianne Storm, and Marilyn Swain.

I want to give a special thanks to coach Louderback for putting up with my overzealous attitude and always believing in me; to Bud Little, who taught me to write; to Mark Pettengill for trusting me; to my editor, Connie Kallback, for tons of hard work and encouragement; and to all the Foothill Players, who have helped build the proud tradition of Cougar football.

About the Author

Jerry Vallotton spent 14 years playing football and 19 years coaching it. He has been a head coach, offensive and defensive coordinator, and has coached all individual positions. (His emphasis is O-line.) "Coach Val" has also been published in several coaching magazines. He has worked as a consultant and clinician since publishing his first article in 1993. His website has been a hub of information for many doublewing coaches. See www.doublewing.org for other coaching helps.

Foreword

I have known Jerry Vallotton all of my adult life. We played football together at Azusa Pacific University. We have coached against each other in our early careers in Los Angeles County. I have observed him as both an assistant and head football coach, and I am honored to have him as a vital part of our staff at Foothill High School.

As a coach he is hard working, loyal, committed, caring, learned, eager, painfully honest, and obnoxiously thorough. He is also an excellent role model, a godly man, and a devoted father and husband.

As high school football coaches, we should be in this business for young people, but what can keep us ticking through the tough times is our relationship with fellow coaches. We are in a unique profession. Who else can empathize with us about euphoric highs and the draining lows; the battles with budgets, administrators, boosters, and second guessers: sharing the strain that coaching can be on our families and wallets? After all, for several months out of the year we spend more time with other coaches than with our families. I am truly blessed to work in this brotherhood with Jerry Vallotton.

Football coaches come in three categories:

1. those who do what they do and will not change for anybody,
2. those who do what they do and are always open to a little change, and
3. those who are always looking for change.

If you are in the second or third categories you will enjoy taking a look at this offense.

I like to consider myself a student of the game of football. After running the Toss, I am in utter awe of the success that we and others have had with it. It is an extremely simple offense to run, yet gives the appearance of a complex system.

In addition to all of this, the following of the Toss is "cultish." Our players and fans love this system. I feel like a salesman for a wonderful product, but we know of no football program that has been sold on this package and failed. It sounds too good to be true, but I recommend that you examine this system; it could vitalize or revitalize your career. It has mine.

Mark Pettengill
Head Football Coach
Foothill High School
Redding, California

About This Book

While attending Azusa Pacific University, a small private college near Pasadena, my friends and I dedicated ourselves to both academic and athletic pursuits. It was there we began grooming ourselves for our life-long passion, which also doubled as our occupation: teaching and coaching.

Soon after graduating, we went our separate ways, although we settled close enough to compete against each other, coaching at our respective high schools. We were young, ambitious, and highly competitive. We searched for the best strategies we could find.

That search brought some of us in touch with Don Markham, a highly successful coach with a long list of championship teams. It was Markham's influence that helped us begin winning our own championships. As a coach, I first got involved with "The Toss" scheme (Markham's trademark) by trying to coach against it. After getting run over by it, I, too, became a big fan.

Well, it's been a few years now and my college buddies are spread out all over the country. Ironically, many are still close. Our careers have been filled with ups and downs, but one thing has remained constant: We have all discovered that what Don Markham scribbled down years ago was pure genius. His offensive packages have been an unlimited source of productivity.

We—the coaches and football team—at our school have enjoyed the fruits of the plan enormously. I have written this book in order to explore and record all of the intricate details. In doing so, it has helped me teach it better. My desire is to have exhaustive documentation of the offense for our assistant coaches, as well as any other coach who is still on a quest for the perfect plan.

At the writing of this book, "The Toss" is being used primarily by a relatively small number of high schools, and mostly in the state of California. This small band of coaches has another thing in common besides their offense—they are all successful. Now, I have no idea at this time how popular this attack may become. What I do know is that the coaches who use it now have no intention of dropping it.

As I have observed the development of this offense, both as a coach who tried to defend against it, and as one who helped install it, I have seen a varied reaction from coaches when they see it. Many are very skeptical, thinking it is just too strange to implement. Still others attempt to borrow only bits and pieces and become disillusioned by their failure. The same coaches may have visions of grandeur about creating their own innovative attack. I was guilty of all these before I converted to "The Toss." I think you can be too eclectic. This is especially true of young coaches who have not yet decided which direction they will go on offense, defense, or just general coaching philosophy. Experimentation is good, but it can be very painful. Trial and error can take a toll on coaches as well as players. Whole programs have crumbled, or at the very least experienced severely stunted growth because the head coach would not settle on a single sound concept—especially on offense.

Football is a game. In my opinion, it is the world's greatest sport because it is so intricate. On the other hand, it is very simple. The paradox of working on the depth and width of all areas, while not forgetting the simplicity of blocking, tackling, and other foundational elements makes coaching football a great challenge. If you look around at successful football programs, you will find coaches who have found offensive schemes that work. They have a single-mindedness when it comes to how to attack a defense. They have bought into something they really believe in. This is half the battle. But whatever the scheme is, it must be considered only after seeing the whole picture.

"There is nothing new under the sun." This is true to a point: There are "new" offenses, but they are actually combinations of old concepts, plays, and formation. It must be the package that wins. And even if you are Bill Walsh, you are unlikely to "invent" the next great football offense that becomes the rage in America. Many coaches have tried, only to fail and drag down their teams with them. What you can do is shop around—call, write, or visit coaches you admire. Weigh them in the balance. Investigate all aspects of their attacks. Talk to your own coaches and players. Think it through, because

About This Book

once you decide, you should lock on and stick with it through the rough waters that will come early on as you introduce your new scheme. As you begin to shape and develop it, you will find a confidence that comes from knowing you have a sound product. The hidden fears of uncertainty will be diminished by the knowledge it has worked for others. There will also be plenty of room for your personal touch in many areas: new techniques, new adjustments, even new plays.

We have experienced all of this in our program. The investment in "The Toss" has paid off a hundredfold. We never could have imagined the results we have achieved from its use. Everything we wished for in an offense has come true and then some. The more we run it, the better we get. The more we coach it, the more we discover its potential. Going from 0-10 to 10-0 and setting the state scoring record is proof to us that we have found the right plan.

It has worked for teams in a variety of settings. Some teams had a winning tradition; some did not. Some had deep talent to draw from, and others did not. Regardless of the situation, the magic of "The Toss" has worked every time. And it will work for you.

Jerry Vallotton

Contents

Foreword—ix
About This Book—xi

PART ONE "THE TOSS"
What It Is & Why It Works

CHAPTER 1. THE SUCCESSFUL HISTORY OF "THE TOSS"   3

Father of the Scheme.............................4
Another "Toss" Leader............................5
Sticking With "The Toss".........................6

CHAPTER 2. THE BASIC THEORY BEHIND THE ATTACK: WHY IT WORKS   7

The 5-Formation Is an Even Set...................7
We Have Toe-to-Toe (Tight) Splits................8
The Fullback Is Set Extremely Close to the Quarterback..8
We Have a Wing in Motion on Every Play...........9
Using One Formation Makes It Difficult to Key
   Tendencies....................................9
Our Cadence Is Always "Ready, Set, Hit, Hit".....10
We Run a Few Plays Perfectly.....................10
Our Blocking Schemes Allow Constant Victory......11
We Utilize Deception to Thin the Defense at the
   Point of Attack..............................12
We Have a Few Basic Adjustments..................13

PART TWO THE FOUR BASIC PLAYS
Toss, Sweep, Cut, & Cross-Toss

CHAPTER 3. "THE TOSS:" THE HUB OF THE WHEEL   19

Backside Blockers Make the Play..................21
The Wing Moves on the First "Hit"................21

CHAPTER 4. THE SWEEP: A NEW LOOK AT AN OLD PLAY 27
   Attacking the Defensive End 29

CHAPTER 5. THE CUT PLAY: THE DISAPPEARING MAN TRICK 33

CHAPTER 6. THE CROSS TOSS: WHEN ALL ELSE FAILS 39
   Timing Is Crucial 41

PART THREE FINE TUNING
Adjustments to the Basics

CHAPTER 7. PLAY TOOL BOX: ROUTINE AND EXTREME 47
   The Dive 47
   The Sneak 47
   No Play/Pass 48
   Tight End Counters 49
   Toss Option 49
   Cut Option 51

CHAPTER 8. THE PLAY ACTION PASSING SCHEME 53
   Toss-Pass 53
   Look-In 54
   Cross-Toss Pass 56
   Scissors Pass 57
   Explode 59
   Explode-X 60
   Near Boot 61
   Far Boot 62
   Pitch Pass 63

CHAPTER 9. WINGS ON: COUNTERING LOADED FRONTS 65
   Green: Wing Shifts Up 65
   Blacks: Wing Shifts Back 68

CHAPTER 10. DOUBLE-TEAM SCHEMES FOR "THE TOSS" 73
   Versus 5-2 73
   Versus 7-2 74
   Versus 6-2 76
   Versus 7-1 76
   Versus 6-5 77

PART FOUR CHANGING THE LOOK, KEEPING THE CONCEPT
Variations & Strategies

CHAPTER 11. ADVANCED DOUBLE WING RUNNING PLAYS   83
  Quarterback Blast............................83
  Reverse....................................85
  Keeper.....................................86
  Dive-Cross-Toss Fake.......................87
  Toss Sweep.................................87
  Toss Keep..................................89
  Guard Trap.................................89
  Yo-Yo Toss.................................90
  Wing to I Toss.............................91

CHAPTER 12. ADVANCED DOUBLE WING PASSING PLAYS   93
  Toss Keep Pass.............................93
  Scissors Deep..............................95
  Speed Pass.................................97
  Reverse Pass...............................98
  A Final Note on Personnel..................98

CHAPTER 13. I-FORMATION: CHANGE CAN BE GOOD   99

CHAPTER 14. I-FORMATION RUNNING PLAYS: FEATURE BACK   105
  I-Toss....................................105
  I-Cut.....................................106
  I-Sweep...................................108
  I-Trap....................................109

CHAPTER 15. I-FORMATION PASSING PLAYS: FEATURE RECEIVER   111
  I-Trap Pass...............................112
  I-Scissors................................113
  I-Pitch Pass..............................113
  Fade......................................115
  Comeback..................................116
  Slant.....................................116
  Hitch.....................................118

CHAPTER 16. STACK-I FORMATIONS: BRING DOWN THE HAMMER   119
  Stack-Toss................................120

Stack-Switch 120
Stack-Sweep 122
Stack-Cut 123
Stack-Lead 123
Stack-Trap 125
Stack-Tight End Reverse 126
Stack-Trap Pass 127

PART FIVE THE PLAYERS
The Ideal, Training, & Motivation

CHAPTER 17. PERSONNEL: THE MOVING PARTS 131

Special Qualities Are Not Needed 131
Building the Perfect Toss Team 132
Position-by-Position 133

CHAPTER 18. MAKING WHAT YOU HAVE BETTER 137

Training 137
Competition 138
Motivation 140

PART SIX
WHERE THE RUBBER MEETS THE ROAD
Implementing Schemes, Evaluations, & Drills

CHAPTER 19. PRACTICE SCHEMES 145

The Typical Week: Friday to Friday 145
Monday: Review, Preparation, Light Practice 146
Tuesday: Let's Go to the Video 146
Wednesday: More Videos, Drills, Simulations 148
Thursday: Dress Practice 149
Game Night 150

CHAPTER 20. POST GAME: EVALUATION OF YOUR DEFENSE 153

Game Drive Chart 155
Formation-Play Chart 156
Individual Offense Chart 157
Individual Mistake Chart 158
Praise Charts 159
Coaching Error Notes 160

Personnel Adjustments 161
Formation/Play Adjustments 162
Individual Drill Chart by Position 163

Chapter 21. Drills   165

Offensive Line Agility Drills...................... 165
Z-Series Drills................................. 167
Sled Drills: 6-Point Progression 169
Live Progression Drills........................... 170
Combination Drills 171
Log-Block Drills................................ 172
Bag Series Drills................................ 173
Down and Dirty Drills........................... 174
One-on-One Drills.............................. 175
Additional Quarterback and Running Back Drills...... 176

Chapter 22. Buying Into the Total Package   183

Ball Control.................................... 184
Commitment to Perfection 185
The Four-Down Concept......................... 186
Play Selection................................... 186
Working "The Toss" Play 186
Running Trick Plays.............................. 187
Running "The Toss" to the Sideline 187
Scoring.. 188
Running Versus Passing........................... 188
Team Buy-In of the Plan 190

Appendix   191

Index   197

Part One

The Toss

What It Is & Why It Works

Chapter 1

THE SUCCESSFUL HISTORY OF THE TOSS

Upon this point, a page of history is worth a volume of logic.
—Oliver Wendell Holmes Jr.

Trends come and trends go. This is especially true when it comes to offensive strategy. One reason for constant change is the need to counter excellent defenses, which adapt to stop new offensive maneuvers. Other trends are invented by innovative geniuses. Coaches are professional plagiarizers and readily incorporate the successful ideas of others. So when a change in status quo occurs and a new scheme gains success, several coaches will begin trying it. Some borrow bits and pieces; others buy into it full bore. Each adds a few personal variations which enhance the offense as it spreads throughout the country.

"The Toss" is no exception. We call this offense "The Toss" for lack of a better name. Some refer to it as "The Blast." It appears to be similar to the "Countertray" made popular by the Washington Redskins. It has within it some of the same characteristics as the popular Wing-T offense. It can be run out of several formations. Early in its formative years it was run mostly from I-formation sets. Recently, the switch to a double tight end, double wing set (Diagram 1-1) has greatly increased its potency.

It is difficult to predict how fast or to what extent an idea will grow, but from what I have experienced in the past few years with the teams that have gone to "The Toss," many others will begin to desire the successful production that it has provided to the teams which employ this strategy.

```
              Left              Right
              ────              ─────
              ODD               EVEN

 9       7  5   3   1   0   2   4   6        8
         ⓠ  O   O   □   O   O   ⓠ
       ② WB  #6         ① QB        *5  ④ WB
         Left                           Right
                        ③ FB
```

DIAGRAM 1-1   5 FORMATION—DOUBLE TE, DOUBLE WING

Father of the Scheme

To give a brief overview of the short history of "The Toss," I will begin with Don Markham. Don is the father of this scheme. It dates back to the 1970s when Markham was coaching at Los Angeles Baptist High School. He began using the technique of pulling the entire backside of the offensive line (guard and tackle).

Since then Coach Markham has been enormously successful wherever he has been, which includes Colton, Bishop Amat, and Romona High Schools in southern California. His collection of league championships, playoff victories, and point totals speak volumes about both the offense and his ability to coordinate it. He recently coached at Bandon High School in Oregon. He took a small, losing team to the state playoffs several years in a row, and racked up some unbelievable scoring statistics. Don then went to Bloomington High School in southern California, and there his team not only smashed the California scoring record, but went on to demolish the national scoring record set by Big Sandy High School of Texas in 1975. Don's 1994 Bloomington High School team scored 880 points in 14 games! That's an average of 62 points per game: The team racked up 6,439 yards, close to 460 yards per game. Greg Oliver, Bloomington's feature back, scored 352 points to become California's all-time season leader. What makes this even more incredible is that Bloomington was 1–9 in 1993.

Another "Toss" Leader

Another great innovator in the progression of "The Toss" is Phil Bravo, formerly the head coach at Whittier Christian High School. Phil has been a close follower of Markham and has successfully installed a combination of new and old ideas to win his share of championships in both league and sectionals. He has since moved to Centaurus High School in Colorado and has continued frequenting playoff games there as well.

Many other schools have run this offense with great success. In fact 10 out of 21 California state rushing record holders have come from teams running this offense. Mazio Royster, Eric Bieniemy, Leonard Russell, Ryan Knight, and David Dotson are a few names that appear in the state record books. At Foothill, we had three backs sharing the same backfield (all juniors) who each rushed for close to 1000 yards in the same year.

To my knowledge, only one school has experienced a losing season while running this offense, and that was our team at Foothill High School. We went 0-10, but we had only players through their junior year because we were a brand new school. It is interesting to note that we still average more than 300 yards per game (most on the ground) against a full varsity schedule.

SENDING OUT A POSSE OF BLOCKERS.

Sticking With "The Toss"

I am proud to close this chapter with a happy ending, at least for our program. Mark Pettingill, head coach and offensive coordinator (formerly at Bassett High School) enjoyed a total turn around. Mark and I really struggled that year when we didn't win a game in ten tries, but we remained confident that we were doing the right thing by sticking with "The Toss."

The next year we went 10-0 in league play, winning our school's first league championship. We also set three all-time California state records. We achieved the third best state scoring average by totaling more than 56 points per game. We also set the differential record (462). And most importantly, we set the all-time state scoring record (for a 10-game regular season) with a 564 point total. We ended up 11-1 overall, and finished ranked third in the state in our division. We are obviously ecstatic about the results this offense has produced. We are certain that any team that decides to run it and dedicates itself to the following concepts will be successful.

Chapter 2

THE BASIC THEORY BEHIND THE ATTACK: WHY IT WORKS

I want to seize fate by the throat.
—Beethoven

Before I begin illustrating why this offensive attack is so effective, I want to say a word about formations. This offense has been run out of several different formations. This offense was originally run from mostly I-formation sets, with or without motion. This would include pro, slot, double tight end's, and tight wing. It has also been effective using a stack-I set with some variation. Some teams have even used a one-back formation with a double slot or double flanker combination.

All of these different formations change the way the basic offense is blocked, and/or which plays are selected. By changing formations and plays, you discover creative alternatives as you develop your scheme. However, we have banked on the theory that less is better when it comes to formations. For this reason, I will first be describing everything out of what we call the "5-formation" (Diagram 1-1). In the past few years, teams that have converted to this set have achieved amazing results. Here is an extensive list that covers why this attack works so well.

The 5-Formation Is an Even Set

Having a balanced set with two tight ends and two wings forces defenses to also play a basic even set. This prevents them from playing their usual strength-oriented defense. It also cuts down on a number of stunts and blitzes the defense could use based on formation. It dictates what they can and cannot do and also takes them out of their game plan. The even set also makes it easy to determine how they will defend you, therefore making it easier to set up blocking schemes.

We Have Toe-to-Toe (Tight) Splits

From tight end to tight end, we set up zero space between linemen. By having such a tight formation, we again force the defense into playing our game. They must squeeze down into the box (tackle to tackle). This may seem as if it's an advantage for the defense because of the clogging effect it has on runs inside the tackles, but you must consider what this offense wants to do.

Our first priority is to run "The Toss" (Chapter 3) off tackle. By having the defense bunched up they can easily be downblocked and/or walled up in droves, therefore creating big seams or running lanes.

Here's another reason tight splits work in our favor: They make it very difficult to see the ball carrier through the line of scrimmage.

The formation has also proven to be blitz proof. Many defenses have tried to penetrate the gaps in an attempt to disrupt the pulling and running lanes—but it simply does not happen.

The Fullback Is Set Extremely Close to the Quarterback

Our fullback is so closely aligned, his head is set just inches away from the quarterback's rear end. This alignment has proven to be very effective because it enhances the angle the fullback uses to kick out the defensive end. The angle is an inside-out (head in the hole) force that is the essential weapon in opening up "The Toss" play.

We also run a short trap (Chapter 5) in which the fullback comes in front of the quarterback and follows the pulling guard. By having the fullback tight, it makes it difficult for linebackers to see him until it's too late.

We Have a Wing in Motion on Every Play

One wing will always be in motion across the formation, regardless of the play. He is already set in a three-point stance just outside the tight end's hip (and should be able to touch him). The wings are set at a slightly inward angle. They are also as close to the line of scrimmage as legally possible, with their helmets' ear holes in the tight end's hip.

The wing's motion route takes him in an arch behind the fullback. He motions in a half-shuffle, half-jogging action. He should keep his head and shoulders slightly twisted toward the quarterback at all times, with his hands up, ready to receive the pitch (or fake pitch). We feel this is to our advantage because of the visual deceptiveness of the motion as a decoy.

No matter how disciplined a defense is, they must always take into account the wing motion every play. We also feel the motion gives the wing a great advantage when he does get the ball. He actually gets a running start that allows him to hit the line of scrimmage at full speed! Another added bonus is the motion across an already crowded formation into a trips (three receivers: tight end, wing, motion wing) set makes it a real pain when trying to play man-to-man defense. The wing simply gets lost in the crowd.

Using One Formation Makes it Difficult to Key Tendencies

When we scout an opponent's offense we chart everything. But, what we really utilize is the chart on tendency by formation. Many offensive schemes are blatantly simple to read because they run certain plays when they are in certain formations.

With our scheme, it is impossible to predict what play is to be run based on the formation used. We look the same at the line of scrimmage. We motion the same way on every play. We even look the same (or at least similar) at the onset of each play's action. This becomes vitally important because when you run only four or five different plays all game, you must keep the defense guessing and not allow them to anticipate or read until the play is into full action, and it is too late for them to stop you.

Our Cadence Is Always: "Ready, Set, Hit, Hit"

We feel our offensive line gets off quicker than any other team's. Now this may not be surprising that we beat defenses to the punch, but we feel we are also faster than any other offense because we always go on two. Our cadence never changes from "ready, set, hit, hit." For this reason our offensive linemen do not hesitate. They do not think; they can be free and confident that they will always be correct on the snap count.

This may sound ridiculous to some who feel you must keep the defense guessing in order to beat them to the punch, but we have found we do better when we know the count. This also sets up our "freeze sneak." The quarterback will tap the center's rear end when he's ready, and the center and quarterback will surge forward while the rest of the offense will remain frozen. This is highly effective because defensive linemen are trained to go on movement, not sound.

So, if our linemen (who are always set immediately in a three-point stance) do not move, the defensive linemen will not move either! The defense actually gets lulled to sleep, so to speak. They get comfortable with going on two for so long that they get careless and are not set!

Another play we use off this is "no-play," which is just what it says, a non-play. We set up as normal, but the quarterback will bark out "ready, set, hit, hit, hit" and so on until one of two things happens:

1. He gets the defense to jump for an easy five-yard penalty, or
2. he is convinced they won't jump, in which case the motion wing calls time-out.

This play is for a third down, short yardage situation, or even forth and short, because you will either gain a first down or you will use a time-out at a time you would use one anyway.

We Run a Few Plays Perfectly

There are two schools of thought when it comes to running plays. One says to keep the defense guessing by utilizing various formations with a variety of different plays. The other emphasizes execution of a few plays in order to run them flawlessly. The stress is put on the performance of the offense, not the confusion of the defense. We obviously fall into the latter school of thought. We run the same four or five running plays hundreds and hundreds of times throughout the week.

We feel we gain a tremendous amount of confidence because we eliminate doubt and confusion through hours and hours of preparation that goes into only a few plays. Having a few plays also gives us time to focus an intense amount of attention on every detail of each play. We simply do not tolerate *any* mistakes in *any* area of *any* play.

You may say that our scheme would create low morale in practice because of the mundane routine of repetition with little variety. But players do not get tired of practicing if what you are doing is successful. There is nothing in football more exciting than scoring a touchdown, and scoring brings success, and success brings excitement!

Our Blocking Schemes Allow Constant Victory

In most offenses there will be several plays designed to depend on one or two blockers moving their defensive opponent away from the point of attack. This type of play creates great opportunity for failure because it is based on the performance of a few key individuals instead of the entire team. We, however, use a team-attack concept. Our scheme utilizes most, if not all, eleven men at the point of attack. If a player is not involved in the point of attack, he is drawing away defenders by being a decoy. We depend heavily on down blocking (or angle blocking) and double teams.

We also use a trap or kick-out blocks. And our most effective blocking concept is that by pulling the entire backside (guard and tackle), we create mismatches (Chapter 3) by using the advantage of angles: two-on-one situations with the defense being outmanned at the point of attack. We simply do not need any one lineman to take his man head up and depend on sheer force to move him one way or the other. I will discuss this further as we get into individual plays.

We Utilize Deception to Thin the Defense at the Point of Attack

By having our "Toss" play as the hub of our scheme—a play which we attack with nine guys at or near the point of attack, we force defenses to overreact in order to stop us. If they begin to concentrate their efforts in one area, they become vulnerable to counters and play action. We try to take full advantage of this and take what they give us, rather than forcing the issue in one area.

We demand good fakes from our tight ends in decoy pass routes. We ask our backs to follow through on fakes for at least 10 yards. We push this concept hard in practice. We stress crisp ball handling by our quarterback, and even ask him to carry out a fake throwing motion to coincide with our tight end's decoy route.

By utilizing deception on every play, we actually minimize the defenders at the point of attack. If we have one fake, we can influence three or four potential tacklers away from the play. If we have two or three fakes, you can figure we have the defense's eleven men all over the field.

LOOKING FOR THE BIG YARDS

One point should be mentioned about our opponents having difficulty simulating this offense in practice. We have coaches tell us it was next to impossible to simulate our plays during practice with a scout squad. If a team cannot run it effectively during practice, then the defense never gets a real good look at it, which really puts a crimp on their preparation, not to mention their ability to play against us.

We Have a Few Basic Adjustments

I have read books that teach literally hundreds of blocking scheme adjustments. Either they are pre-called in the huddle, or they use a complicated check-off system at the line of scrimmage. These systems, I'm sure, are well thought out and very effective when they work, but unless you have the practice hours of a Division 1 university, or a professional training camp, I cannot see being able to execute many of these blocking scheme adjustments with any amount of efficiency. We depend very little on our high schoolers to decipher and adjust on their own. We do, however, adjust.

The first way we want to adjust is to run a different play. It sounds simple, but with our offense it is amazing how just going down the short play list opens things up. For instance, if we have attempted to establish our "Toss," but have made little or no progress, then we run a sweep or cut (trap) and almost always gain big yardage. We will then go back to "The Toss" and the defensive will usually open up. Once a defense moves to adjust to an area, it opens itself somewhere else. Even if the defense does not change formation, it changes its thinking. The defense begins anticipating a play and flies to stop it. They over pursue and a counter action kills them.

Another way we adjust is simple whole line or direct area blocking changes. I will discuss all of these as we get to each play, but by way of introduction I will mention the basic concepts.

If we play against an odd front, we will run "base," which means we will use double teams at the point of attack. If we see that the defense is slanting, shifting, using extensive blitz schemes, or running an even front, we will then make adjustments to our "seven" technique, which calls for down blocking (angle blocks) on the play side.

Two other adjustments may be used when we run "The Toss." Teams may widen out a group of defenders beyond our tight end in order to counter the mismatch created by our pulling backside. We have our wing call "tunnel" and we alter our scheme by blocking out with our wing and tight end and have others go up the seam (tunnel). If a defense decides to go to a goal-line defense and put the defensive end head-up or inside our wing, or they decide to slant the defensive end on a hard "crash" mode to nullify our fullback's kickout, we have our wings call "window" (wing down), and one wing proceeds to take out the defensive end with a down block. The fullback adjusts by going up field after the next most dangerous defender.

Another possible adjustment that can be used is changing the alignment of our wings. We can make a change during the huddle or the wing can switch alignment on his own. If we call "wings on" (Diagram 2-1), the wing will line up normal at the line of scrimmage; but on "ready," he will shift up to the line of scrimmage just outside the tight end. This wreaks havoc with defensive ends because they're in a bind with the wing's down block (window). If the defensive end hops outside the wing to adjust, we will have the wing block out (tunnel) and a seam is created inside. The wing needs to decoy his alignment on other plays so he does not begin to give away keys by formation.

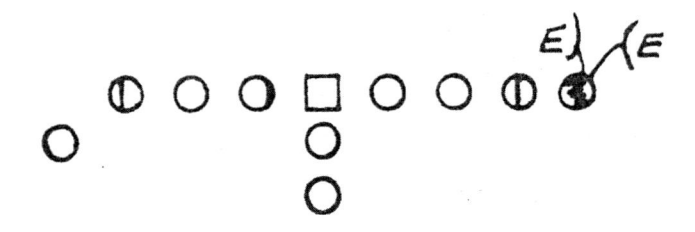

DIAGRAM 2-1   WINGS-ON FORMATION

These adjustments are simple and easy to use. We practice these from day one. We do not have to reinvent entire blocking schemes each week. Some offenses spend hours of vital practice time working on each play versus an opponent's four or five different defensive fronts. This detracts from efficiency. The offense is in a constant state of doubt, and doubt causes hesitation, and hesitation destroys offensive effectiveness.

These factors are why we feel this is one of the most prolific offenses today. It works because of this basic premise. It is a *team*-offensive concept, it is not personnel dependent. Obviously, the better personnel you have, the greater the results. However, this scheme can be effective with average personnel in some, or all positions. At the high school level this becomes important because of the fluctuation of quality from year to year. In other words, if you can't recruit, you must utilize to the maximum what you have. If you're constantly switching offenses to fit your personnel, you are lessening your effectiveness, because you lack consistency. The greatest advantage to this offense is that it can work, and work well regardless of your players' speed, size, or ability.

Part Two
The Four Basic Plays

Toss, Sweep, Cut, & Cross-Toss

Chapter 3

"The Toss:" The Hub of the Wheel

The strength of twenty men. . . .
—Shakespeare

Every offense has "The Play." "The Play" refers to the one individual play that is essential to establishing the rest of the offensive scheme. In the wishbone, for instance, it is a must to run "The Dive" successfully. Without it the quarterback's run or running back's pitch action will not flourish. The same applies to this offense. Without the toss play, "The Toss" offense does not work. That is not to say that using counters and alternate plays will not help, but conceptually you must make the defense see and defend the toss play first. Even if you gain only a few yards the first couple of times you run it, the idea is to lay a foundation for the entire scheme to work.

This play's success is based on the mismatch premise; that is, have more blockers than there are defenders and you win! (Diagram 3-1)

"The Toss" versus an odd front will use "base" technique (Diagram 3-1). The center will "post" or set the double team. The inside guard will "drive" the other part of the double team. The inside tackle will post, and the inside tight end will drive in the other double team. The goal with these double teams is to drive the man back so far that you also catch the linebackers, and other pursuers in the mess. We give an award to linemen who get off-the-film (OTF's) blocks. We encourage them to play whistle to whistle—driving their opponent 10-15 yards away from the play. This demoralizes defensive linemen and weakens them throughout the game. We also give pancake awards for knocking an opponent flat. A technique we use while double teaming is the "half-man" block. This is using one arm and shoulder to drive against the double teamed man, and picking off others with your free arm and shoulder.

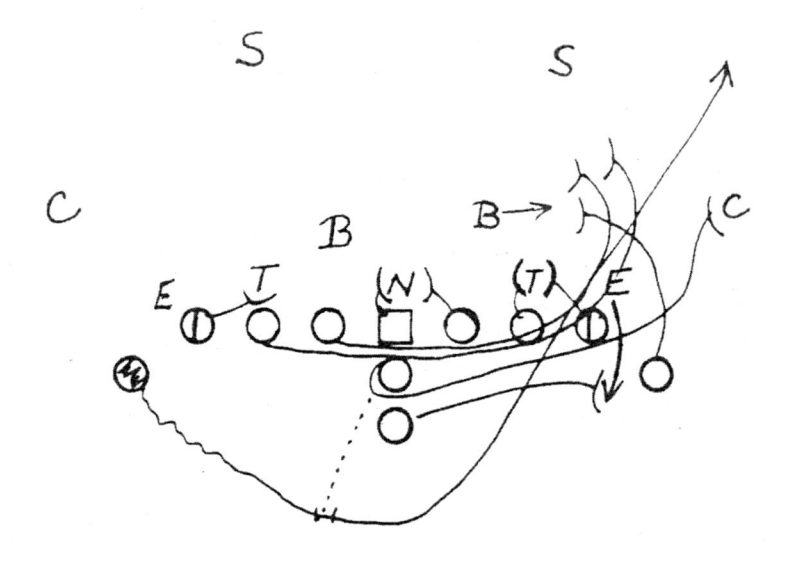

DIAGRAM 3-1 "24 TOSS" (TOSS PLAY—BASE BLOCKING VS. ODD FRONT)

The onside wing loops around the defensive end (sometimes even bluffing a block toward the defensive end to make him hesitate) and cracks back on the nearest linebacker, sealing him inside.

The quarterback reverses out (turning toward the motion wing), keeping the ball next to his inside hip. He then uses a two-handed lob toss, laying the ball in the air so the wing can catch it about chest high on the fly. You must emphasize a soft touch, because if the quarterback pitches the ball too hard toward the wing who is coming at full speed, it will deflect or ricochet off him. The quarterback then completes his rotation and heads up into the hole. He is to wall off the corner back. Even if the quarterback is the worst blocker on the team, all he needs to do is set a pick or screen like in basketball.

Backside Blockers Make the Play

The backside blockers are the ones who really make this play go. The off-guard pulls down the line, staying as close to the line of scrimmage as possible. He looks for daylight and turns up field as soon as he can. He turns up and in. He sets his body facing the backside pursuit two to three yards up field. The off tackle pulls down the line, but is also in charge of cleaning up any penetration leaks along the way. If he does get through, he sets up just up field from the guard, helping to seal the backside.

As far as the safeties (free or strong or both) are concerned, we do not designate anyone in particular to block them. However, if they attack up, the guard, tackle, or onside wing will pick them off if the safeties enter their defensive "tracks."

The off-tight end is the only man who remains home. His job is to take out the defensive tackle. From a three-point stance, he lunges into the thigh pad of the tackle's outside leg. If this cut block is not sufficient, then he will bear crawl forward in order to stay in the legs of the defender. This will tie up the most dangerous backside pursuer.

The fullback is set with his head just inches away from the quarterback's rear end. He takes an inside out route, aiming his head just inside the defensive end. He should explode into the defensive end, kicking him to the outside, creating an off-tackle seam. The defensive end may be stationary, coming on a hard inside rush or driving deep into the back field. The fullback must find him and use his momentum advantage to the fullest.

One other note on the fullback's first step: He must take a cross-over step with his furthest or opposite foot first. This clears his hip away from the quarterback who is rotating toward the pitch man. This takes practice, but it must be done; otherwise, he ends up causing a collision and a possible fumble.

The Wing Moves on the First "Hit"

The wing begins his motion on the first "hit." He receives the ball almost at the top of his arch (Diagram 3-1). With soft hands, he gathers and tucks the ball under his outside arm.

Once the ball is secured, he heads up in the hole. We call our toss play by "45" or "24-Toss" as in 4 back through the 5 hole (see Diagram 1). The hole numbering is relative. It may be in a different spot each time, depending on the blocking action, or the defensive attack. Once he engages into the seam and penetrates the line of scrimmage, he has three options:

1. a radical cut back across the grain,
2. straight up the hash marks, or
3. hit the outside and hope for grass down the sideline (Diagram 3-2).

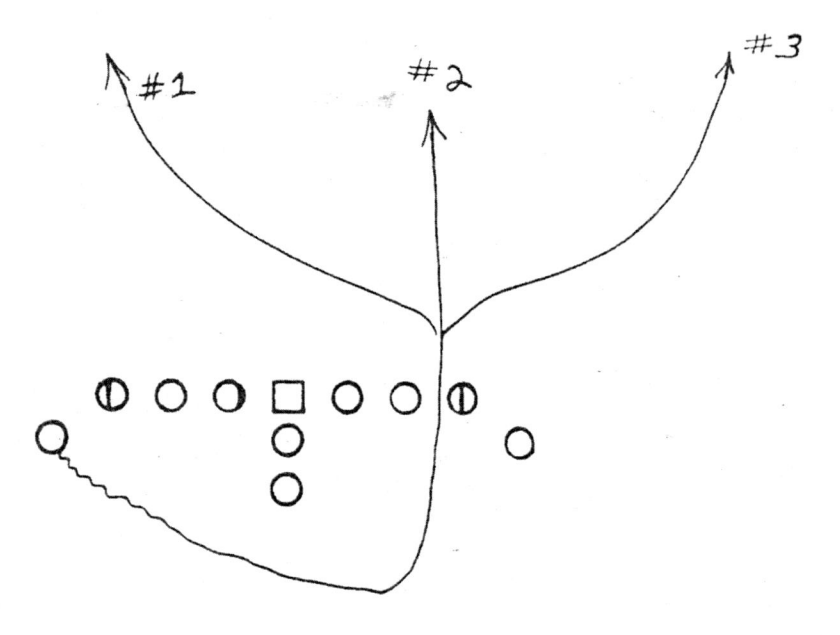

DIAGRAM 3-2 WING'S RUNNING LANES
Note: ONSIDE WING SEES DE SET TIGHT OR IN AN ANGLED STANCE—CALLS "WINDOW."

If the defense depends on movement like slanting, stunts, blitzes, or if they go into an even front, we will utilize our "seven" technique (Diagram 3-3). The center makes the "seven" call, which basically has us abandoning our double teams, and going into a down blocking mode on the onside. Beginning with the center, who snaps, turns, and seals backside (usually the man over the off-guard). The onside guard, tackle, and tight end all "domino" down. The rule is simple—"inside eye or one man down is mine; head up or outside is yours." No matter what front we see, we can block it with "seven."

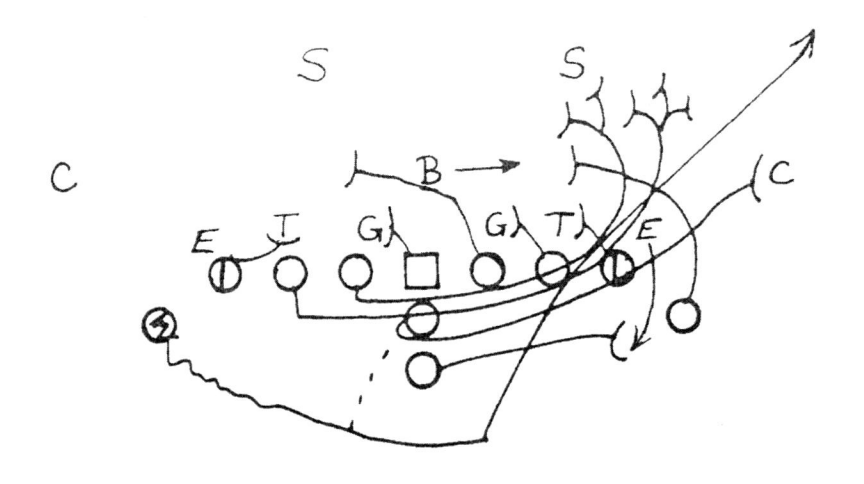

DIAGRAM 3-3   "24 TOSS" (TOSS PLAY—"7" TECHNIQUE VS. EVEN FRONT)

As mentioned previously in Chapter Two, we can utilize "tunnel" (Diagram 3-4) versus a team who stacks defenders to the outside. We can counter teams who use a goal-line, or pinching scheme by using the "window" technique (Diagram 3-5). And finally, we can play with our wing alignment to confuse the defensive end.

We hardly ever fail to gain yards on this play. Because of the stampede effect, we are successful even on plays where we "miss" several blocks. The massive flow of blockers works as a moving force field and even if an opponent slips the first block, he is soon caught up in the wave. We have been in games where we will run this play again and again, switching from left to right, but running the toss play until the defense either stops it and/or overadjusts so much that we can easily run a counter. There is nothing more humiliating than knowing the play is coming, trying everything you can to stop it, and failing over and over again. We call this "smash-mouth" football for obvious reasons.

24 Chapter 3

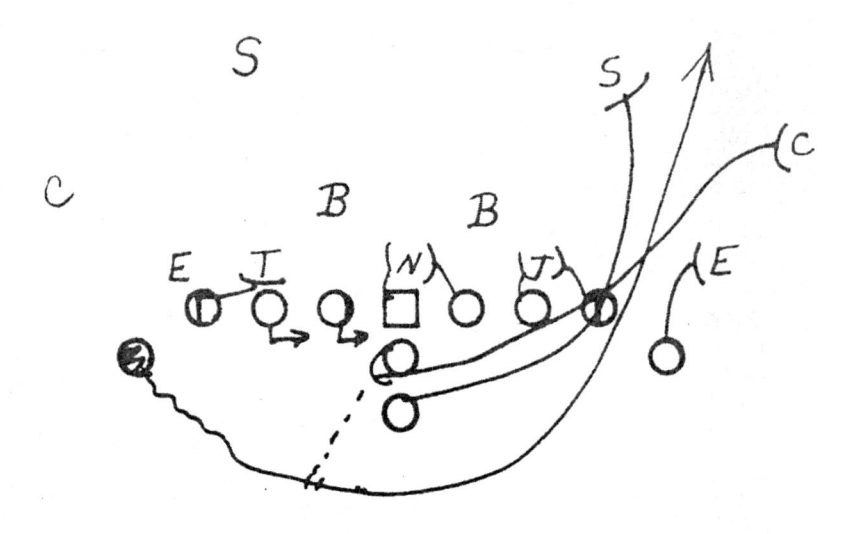

Diagram 3-4 "24 Toss" (Toss Play using "Tunnel" Technique)

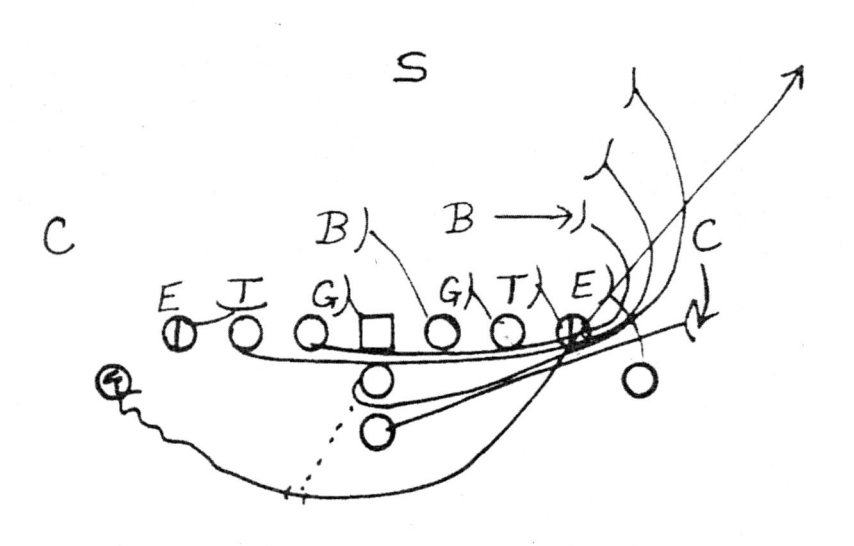

Diagram 3-5 "24 Toss" (Toss Play using "Window" Technique)
Note: Onside wing sees DE set tight or in an angled stance—calls "Window."

"The Toss:" The Hub of the Wheel 25

Step 1: Pre-snap

Step 2: Onside down blocks, backside pulling.

STEP 3: THE PITCH.

STEP 4: THE RUNNER UP INTO THE SEAM.

Chapter 4

THE SWEEP: A NEW LOOK AT AN OLD PLAY

The die is cast.
—Julius Caesar

When you think sweep, you probably think of Vince Lombardi and his Green Bay Packers teams. They made it into an art form. Since then, the sweep has been relegated to the back pages of the play book, due mainly to the improvements in defending against it. Defenses seem to be reacting much faster to the sweep and containing it with well planned perimeter schemes. If your running back is faster than any defender on the perimeter, then you may find success running the sweep, but even then, most teams utilize a quick toss or option set instead of the traditional slowly developing sweep play.

We feel that we can run the sweep and run it well without needing a total speed mismatch. Obviously, the faster your ball carrier, the better the results. We can run the sweep without a speed mismatch because of the effectiveness of "The Toss," the wing's alignment versus the defensive end and the difficulty the defense has in recognizing the sweep soon enough to react (Diagram 4-1).

The play begins with the offside tight end who takes an inside release and runs a corner route. This does several things for us. It draws the backside corner and safety away from the sweep for a while, and if it begins to be ignored, sets up for our play action pass later on.

The tackle will release inside his opponent, head down field to try to pick off a defensive back or linebacker. The off-guard pulls in a shallow track behind the center. He looks to clean up penetration leaks, especially any coming through the on-guard's hole. If he continues down the line, he will turn up and hit the nearest opponent. The center either seals his noseguard by putting his head to the play side hole and rotating his body between the noseguard and the ball carrier, or if it is an even set, then he will "fill block" for the off-guard (Diagram 4-2).

The on-guard pulls out as deep and wide as possible to get beyond the corner back. He attacks the corner back (or whoever is in charge of supporting the outside perimeter). He should run right at the defender, concentrating on the defensive man's belt buckle in order not to get faked out. The on-guard should never leave his feet. He will block the defender wherever he wants to go; if the defender comes inside hard, the on-guard will turn his body and trap the defender inside. If the defender goes hard to the outside, the on-guard will push him out. We train our running backs to see the guard's rear end, and cut in or out accordingly. Blocking corners is fun for guards, they can get many off-the-films (OTF's) or decleaters in this situation!

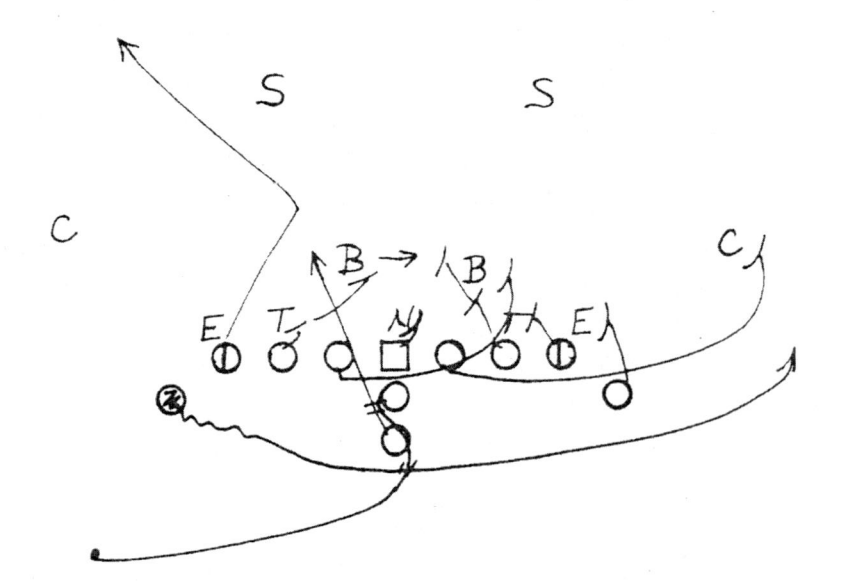

DIAGRAM 4-1 "28 SWEEP" (SWEEP VS. ODD FRONT)

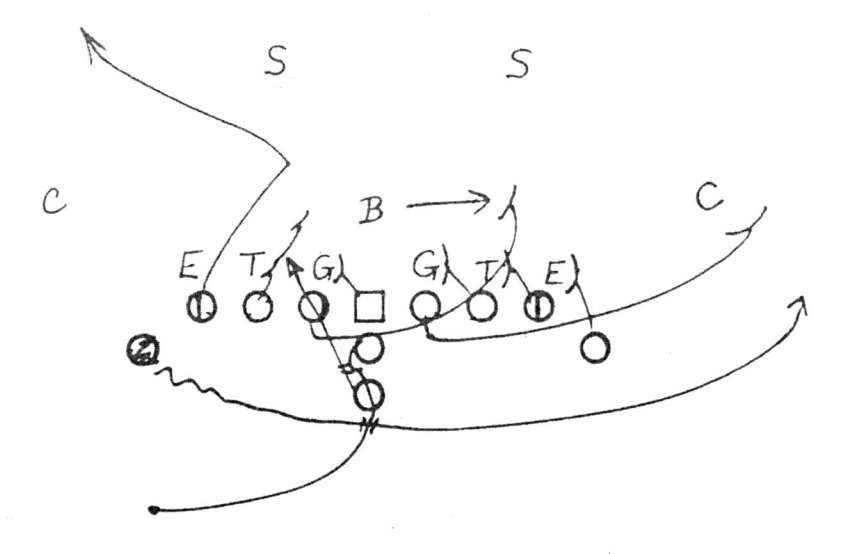

DIAGRAM 4-2 "28 SWEEP" (SWEEP VS. EVEN FRONT)

The onside tackle will downblock; that is, block the next man down. We use a term called "track-blocking," which teaches our linemen to stay on a straight path or track when going after downfield defenders. Not that they will not adjust slightly to go after a straying linebacker, but what we do not want is the common mistake of chasing a single defender all over the field, and end up blocking air.

The tackle, for instance, should block the onside linebacker (versus a 5-2), but there is a good chance he will already be gone in hot pursuit; so the offensive tackle should continue in the same track, and pick off the off-side linebacker or any other defender who crosses his path. The onside tight end down blocks the defensive tackle.

Attacking the Defensive End

The onside wing cracks back on the defensive end. The wing's block is obviously the most important because it takes out the primary containment. Depending on the size mismatch or the wariness of the defensive end, the wing may need to use a few tricks to gain an edge. This is a good situation in which to use the "wings on" alignment, which will give the wing a better angle on a down block if the defensive end stays inside. If the defensive end hops to the outside, then we can use "tunnel," creating a seam similar to "The Toss." If you would rather not be that extreme, then you can have the wing cheat to the outside when he goes to set. Just a few more feet really makes a difference.

Remember, the defensive end has been pounded by the fullback for the last three or four plays by running "The Toss." He has seen the wing loop around him over and over until he begins to disregard the wing. The defensive end—as well as the entire defense—becomes so involved in stopping the off tackle play, they are not ready for the sweep. The wing simply has to aim his head to the up field shoulder of the defensive end and be sure his body is rotated so that he closes the door to outside pursuit lanes.

The fullback fakes dive action (for 10 yards) through the zero or one hole, which should freeze the linebackers for a second. If the linebackers begin to ignore the fake, then it is time to run the cut (Chapter 5).

The quarterback reverses out, fakes to the fullback dive and gives the sweep handoff to the wing. He should then roll away from the sweep action and fake a pass to the tight end who is running a corner pattern. He should watch to see who, if anyone, is coming out with him. If the defense does not follow the quarterback, then he knows he can run play action or a bootleg.

The off-wing begins his motion, but in a slightly flatter route, because he wants to get around the corner as fast as he can. Once the wing receives the handoff, he should locate the lead guard's rear end. The wing should engage into the lead guard's wake, just to his outside hip. The wing will cut according to the guard's block on the corner. The wing can help "set" the block by head faking out and cutting in, or vice versa. We preach a North-South attack. The wing must plant his outside foot and alter his flat, horizontal direction into a hard vertical one as soon as he finds daylight.

This sweep is out of the Wing-T play book. It is not as obvious, nor as slow developing as the traditional fullback lead type. If "The Toss" is the "hard jab" of our scheme, then the sweep is the "right cross." The sweep can be a deadly game breaker if used after the defense has closed in to stop "The Toss."

THE SWEEP: A NEW LOOK AT AN OLD PLAY 31

STEP 1: PRE-SNAP.

STEP 2: FAKE TO FULLBACK; GUARDS PULL.

32 Chapter 4

Step 3: Wing cracks back, gives to wingback.

Step 4: Defense stuck inside; guard leads runner around the end.

Chapter 5

THE CUT (TRAP) PLAY: THE DISAPPEARING MAN TRICK

They have eyes, but they cannot see.
—Psalms 115:5

I am not an expert on visual perception, but I can tell you this: The human brain can concentrate on only one thing at a time. I also know that we often see what our mind tells us it "thinks" it sees, and not what is actually there. Magicians or illusionists make a living fooling our minds into "seeing" what is not there. This same concept is the reason why the short trap or "cut" play is so effective.

Remember, now you have already established your toss and sweep plays, or at least run them enough to influence the defense. You want to create an outside consciousness. The defensive begins seeing the motion man over and over as he goes off-tackle or beyond. They begin to ignore the fullback as he fakes receiving a handoff before the sweep action.

Linebackers start flying to help support the perimeter. Defensive linemen start aggressively penetrating to jam the pulling lanes. Defensive backs struggle to see the wing back's action. Now you are ready to slice or "cut" the defense (Diagram 5-1). The cut is like the left hook in the punch repertoire.

The center will either post the noseguard to set the double-team (versus an odd), or fill block the man over the off-guard (versus an even). The on-guard will drive the double-team in an odd set or down block the linebacker in an even set. Again, he will use the track blocking mode. The on-tackle will dip inside his tackle in an odd set and go after the linebacker (in an even set he will down block the guard's man). The onside tight end will dip inside the defensive end and go after the linebacker. The tackle and tight end will sandwich the onside linebacker versus a 5-2. The onside wing will head downfield and block the nearest safety.

The offside begins with the tight end, who once again runs an inside release corner route in order to influence his man. The tackle will head downfield to pick off a linebacker. The guard will pull down the line of scrimmage, seeking to trap block the defensive tackle at the point of attack. His blocking rule is if the man is in my track (which is just behind the line of scrimmage), he's mine, but if the tackle has overpenetrated (and is now deep into the backfield), turn up field and go after the corner back.

It may seem odd to allow the defensive tackle and defensive end to go unblocked, but they often drive so far out of the picture by overpenetrating, it is just not necessary.

The fullback aims to the off-hip of the quarterback, with his inside elbow up, making a nice pocket for the ball. Once he receives the inside handoff, he plants his foot and cuts laterally down the line behind the center. He engages right behind the pulling guard. He is prepared to cut upfield in the event that the guard has to trap block the defensive tackle, but will continue almost in an off-tackle type direction if the guard is free to attack the corner.

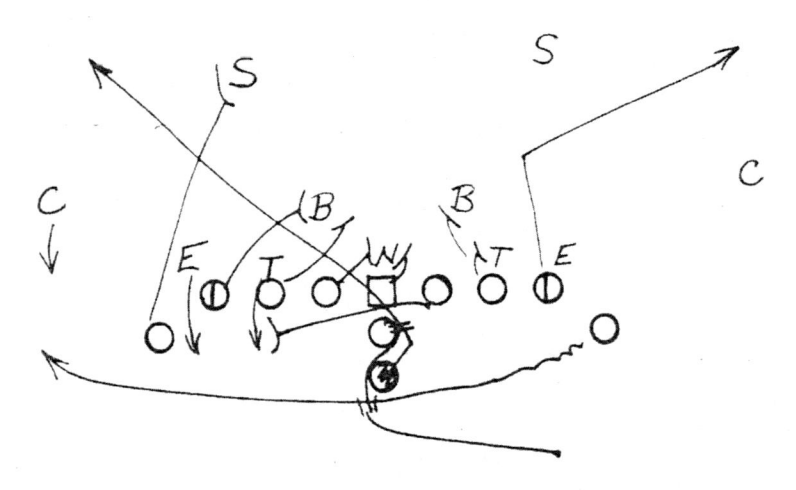

DIAGRAM 5-1   "CUT" (CUT VS. ODD FRONT)

The Cut (Trap) Play: The Disappearing Man Trick

The fullback's action is extremely precise and is done with very tight spacing. Each detail must be worked on to perfection.

The quarterback cannot get deep by stepping backward. He must instead rotate on a dime, holding the ball close to his body as he turns toward the fullback. After completing a half turn and giving a one-handed fake to the wing, he will roll out away from the play and fake a throwing action to the tight end's corner route. This serves to assist in freezing the off-side defensive back and setting up for future play action. The off-wing starts in motion, completes a sweep fake, and continues his decoy action for 10 yards around the corner.

The biggest key to this play is the guard's action. He must be quick to beat the fullback around the center. He must make a split-second decision to block, or not block the defensive tackle. If he does block him, he must really nail him with a head in the hole—"drive-till-you-die"—trap block. If the guard doesn't trap the defensive tackle, he must not hesitate to attack the corner. The previous play selection of toss and sweep will create an over-aggressive defense, which will have begun to abandon normal reservations and responsibilities in order to assist in stopping the outside play (Diagram 5-2).

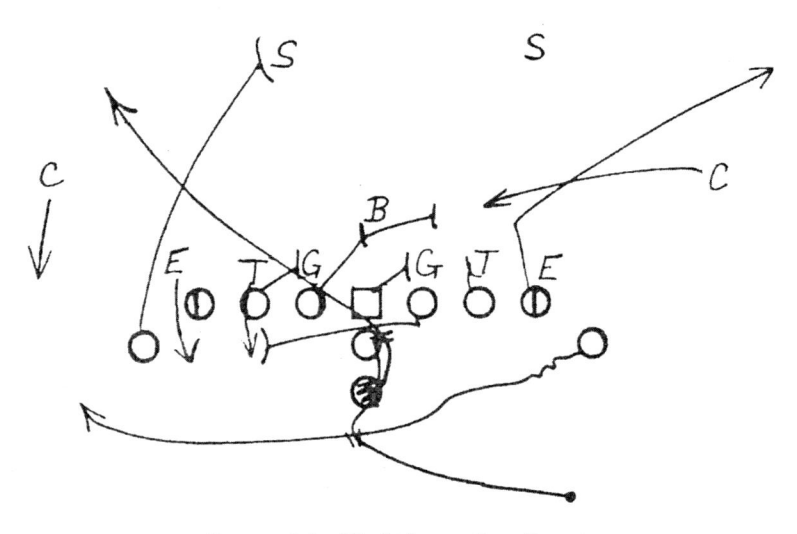

DIAGRAM 5-2   "CUT" (CUT VS. EVEN FRONT)

We have used the cut as a third and long play, almost the way you would a screen. It is amazing to watch the defensive backs chase after the tight end's decoy route, or the quarterback's roll out or fake sweep. We have had times where the play has been blown dead, because the defense tackled either the quarterback or the wing and the referee was fooled!! You may recognize some of the characteristics of the Wing-T trap in this play with, of course, a few variations.

Step 1: Pre-snap.

THE CUT (TRAP) PLAY: THE DISAPPEARING MAN TRICK 37

STEP 2: GUARD PULLS; QUARTERBACK GIVES TO FULLBACK.

STEP 3: WING FAKES SWEEP; QUARTERBACK FAKES BOOTLEG.

STEP 4: DOWNFIELD BLOCKS SET; RUNNER UP THE SEAM.

Chapter 6

THE CROSS TOSS: WHEN ALL ELSE FAILS

Answer a fool according to his folly.
—Proverbs 26:5

There are some times in a game when the defense just has your number. They have done a good job of scouting you, and they seem to have the jump on every play. In these times we like to run our counter—the Cross Toss. It obviously plays off of "The Toss," but can be run in any sequence, because of its counter motion. The quicker the defense, the better this play works. The stay-at-home, or slow defense, will be waiting for it. We teach the linebackers in our defense to read guards and not get fooled by running back fakes, and still they have a tendency to get suckered once in a while. So a defense that doesn't stress guard reads and tries to go with the flow will easily be taken by this play. Even if they do recognize it early, the angles created by our formation serve to wall up the pursuit and kick out the containment.

The play begins with the offside tight end who chop blocks the defensive tackle the same way he does on a regular toss play. The off-tackle pulls, just as he does on the toss, looking to seal up the inside. The off-guard also pulls down the line, but instead of turning up, he is in charge of the defensive end kick out block. The center sets a post on the nose to set up the double-team versus an odd set, or he fill blocks the guard's man versus an even set (Diagrams 6-1 and 6-2).

The onside has the guard driving to finish the double-team versus an odd, or downblocking the linebacker versus an even.

Chapter 6

The tackle posts or downblocks, and the tight end drives the double or downblocks.

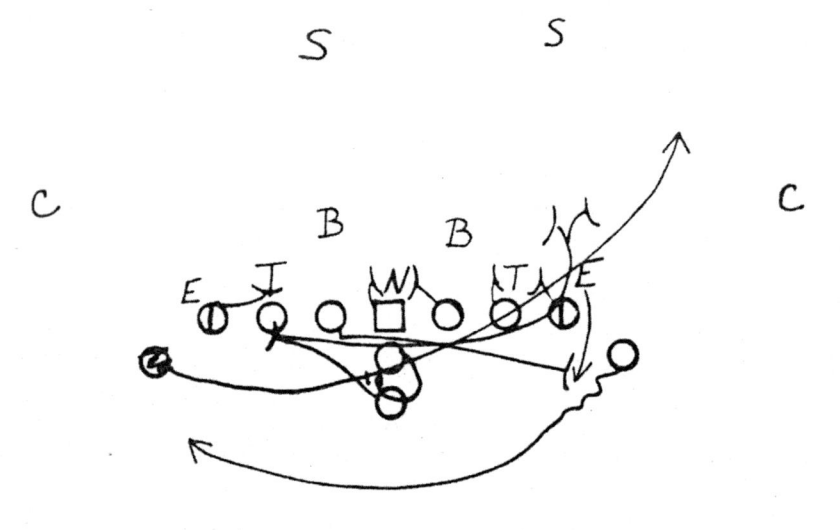

DIAGRAM 6-1   "24 X-TOSS" (X-TOSS VS. ODD FRONT)

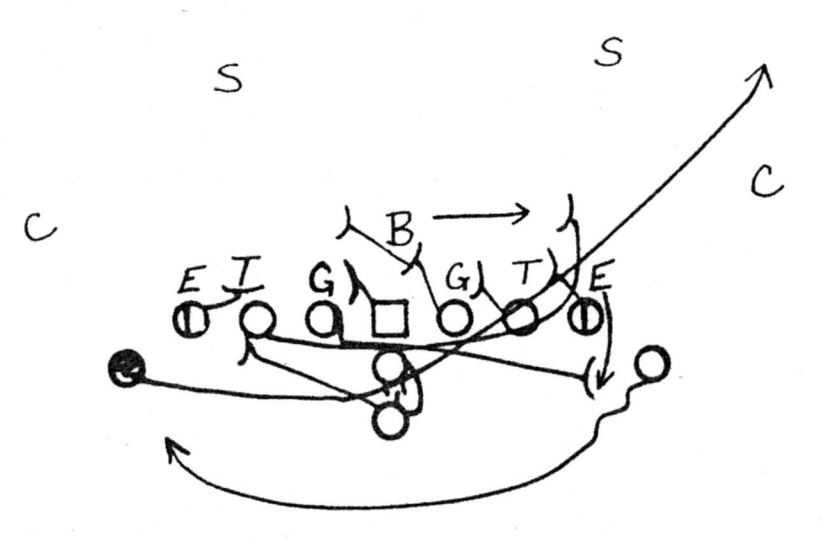

DIAGRAM 6-2   "24 X-TOSS" (X-TOSS VS. EVEN FRONT)

The backfield begins with the on-wing in motioning away from the play side and carrying out a fake toss reception and running a decoy for 10 yards. The fullback also goes away, aiming his head to the inside hip of the tackle. This will serve as a fake toss kick-out route, but is narrower in direction, because he must get out of the oncoming wing's handoff lane. The quarterback will rotate around toward the motion wing, giving a two-handed fake pitch action. He will then pull the ball back, finish a full 360° turn, and give an inside handoff to the oncoming wing. The off-wing will come inside the quarterback (with his downfield elbow up), receive the handoff and follow the guard. The wing will cut accordingly once the defensive end is blocked. His lane choices are limited because of the ultra-flat angle he must use to come under the quarterback. He usually will seek to go outside (lane #3) because of his momentum and the seal inside.

Timing Is Crucial

Timing on this play is crucial. You will be frustrated when you first begin running this play because the wings and fullback all must intersect at the quarterback. Also, by having a wing who is already in motion, the quarterback must really hurry to fake the toss and be back around (completing a 360° turn) in time to meet the other wing, who is coming from the other direction at full speed. One way you can adjust this is to cheat the off-wing's alignment out a little ways. This will delay him just enough to give the quarterback rotation time. However, if the wing is not a naturally fast player, you might not need to do this.

Don't be disappointed if this play flops. It takes only one lazy defensive tackle who decided not to pursue, to botch up a perfectly good play. However, just as is the case with the other plays, when you have run it a few times, it opens up another area of the defense because of a defensive overreaction. Also, when this play does break open, it gains some really big yards, because if the wing can clear the line of scrimmage, he is usually one-on-one with a defensive back in the open field, and if he is even halfway decent, he is going to win that battle most of the time.

Step 1: Pre-snap.

Step 2: The quarterback has rotated 360°, faked to the motion wing and handed off to the other.

The Cross Toss: When All Else Fails   43

Step 3: Guard kicks out defensive end; tackle seals next man.

Step 4: Sustained fakes, sustained blocks; runner headed up the seam.

Part Three

Fine Tuning

Adjustments to the Basics

Chapter 7

Play Tool Box: Routine and Extreme

I think the necessity of being ready increases. Look to it!
—Abe Lincoln

The big four (toss, sweep, cut, cross toss) make up about 85-90 percent of our offense, but like every offense, it's nice to have some extras when you need them. In this chapter, I will give an extensive list of other plays to complement the mainstays.

The Dive

Every offense needs a dive, and we have ours. It is right out of the 1920s. We use a wedge blocking scheme to strengthen the surge forward (Diagram 7-1). This stays with our "team blocking" philosophy. It does not depend on two offensive linemen clearing a path at the point of attack. We simply drive forward and in, joining the linemen at the shoulders. You must stress staying low and "climbing up" from under your man to gain leverage. The tight ends can slip off and crack down on the linebackers as long as they do not loop and create a penetration leak from the outside. This play works well on a "first sound" snap count, especially after going on two the entire game.

The Sneak

As previously mentioned, the "freeze-sneak" is great for goal-line situations. You can also run this sneak with a regular snap count using wedge blocking (Diagram 7-2).

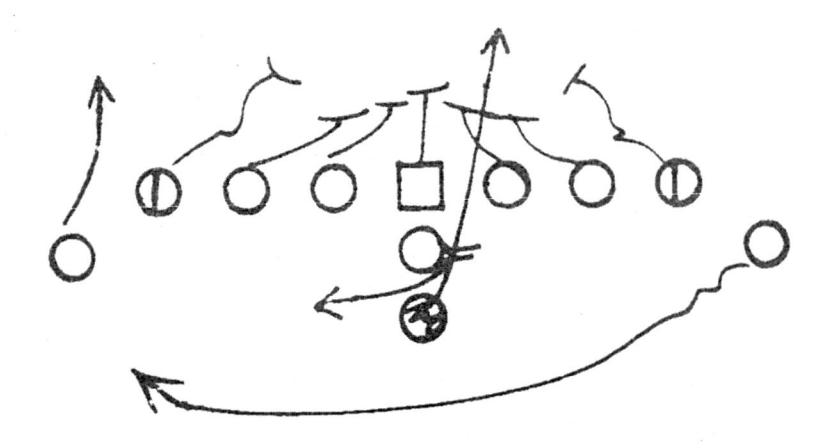

DIAGRAM 7-1 "30 DIVE" (DIVE USING WEDGE BLOCKING)

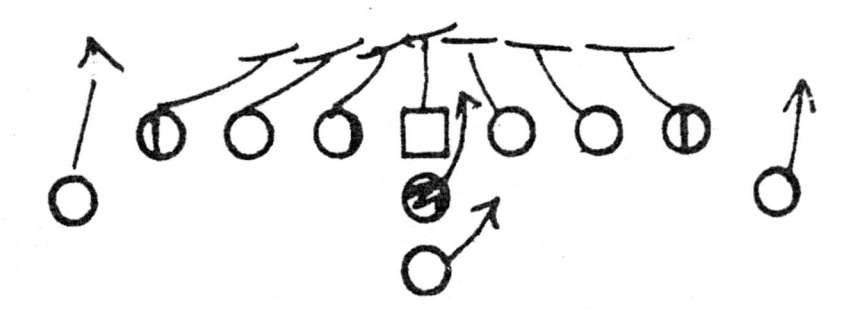

DIAGRAM 7-2 "QB SNEAK ON SOUND" (QB SNEAK USING WEDGE BLOCKING)

No-Play Pass

The no-play no-count play previously mentioned can be turned into a surprise big gain play by having the motion wing (who by the time the snap count has gone to four or five, will be near the sideline) run a streak down the sideline. The quarterback's count will be: "ready, set, hit, hit, hit, hit," and so on—then "set, hit." The second cadence will signal the wing when to go vertical. The quarterback will read the corner's response. Many times after we run the "no-play," the defensive backs will ignore the motion, thinking it is another fake. If the quarterback sees this, he throws the streak. However, if he sees the corner back adjust, he must not sound the second cadence, and call time out. If he sees the corner back come over late, he should throw the ball out of bounds (Diagram 7-3).

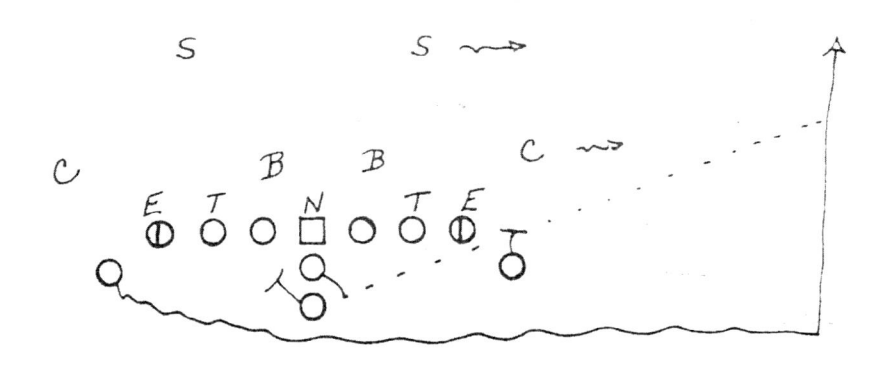

DIAGRAM 7-3 NO-PLAY PASS
CADENCE = "READY, SET, HIT, HIT, HIT, HIT—SET, HIT!"
Note: IF CORNER FOLLOWS, CALL TIME OUT.

Tight End Counters

Another counter play to get your tight end the ball is the 50 and 60 cuts (Diagram 7-4). It is similar to the fullback cut, but the tight end loops back behind the quarterback for a backward handoff and cuts off the guard's block. The onside wing loops around the defensive end to go upfield. The fullback aims to miss the tight end's pull, but tight enough to block the pursuing defensive end.

Toss Option

If your quarterback is a good ball carrier, you can work in the toss keep or toss option series. The toss keep (Diagram 7-5) action is just like the regular toss, but the quarterback rotates, keeps the ball and heads up into the hole. The motion wing trails the same way an option tailback would, keeping a 4×4 (4 yards deep, by 4 yards wide) relationship to the quarterback. Instead of blocking the corner back, we option him.

50   Chapter 7

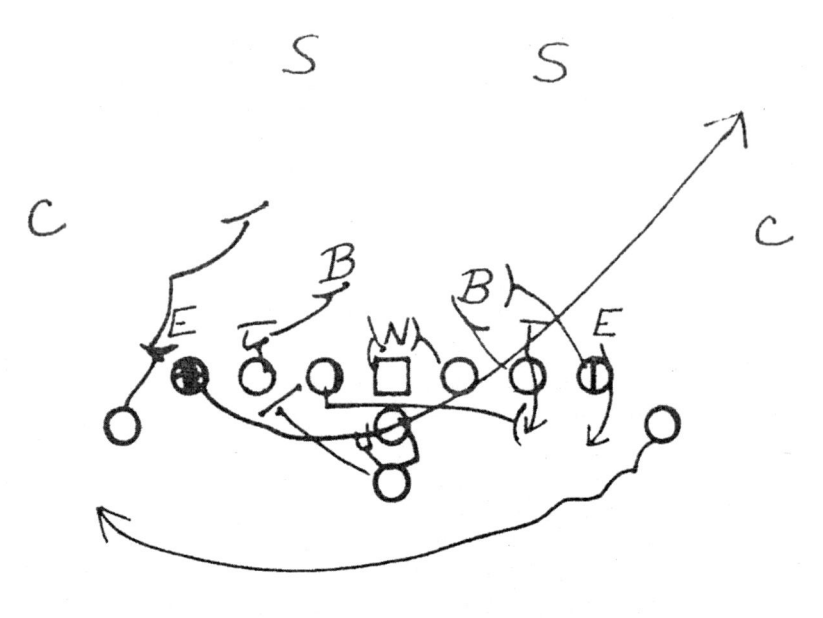

DIAGRAM 7-4   "60 CUT" (TE CUT)

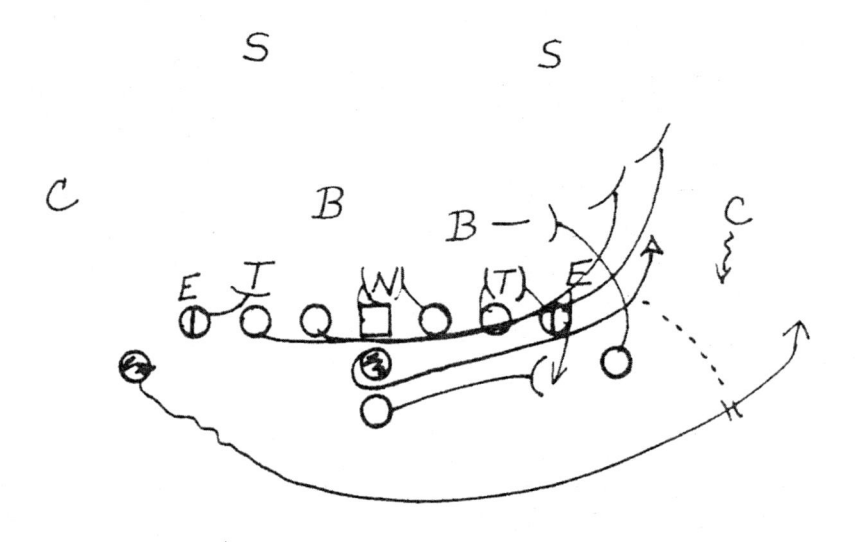

DIAGRAM 7-5   TOSS KEEP OR OPTION

PLAY TOOL BOX: ROUTINE AND EXTREME 51

The quarterback toss option calls for a definite pitch. Consequently, the quarterback should drive into the corner back's inside shoulder, making him commit and then laying a soft pitch to the trailing wing.

Cut Option

Another option that can be a lot of fun is off of the fullback cut play. The play is identical, except the motion wing continues upfield staying in a 4×4 trail behind the fullback (Diagram 7-6). We again option the corner (or whoever attacks the fullback first.)

I am sure some of these sound a bit wacky, especially after preaching the blood and guts of grinding out the basic four plays. However, these, like any other counter or trick plays are meant to be used with the element of surprise, and what better way to set up a shock than to establish a methodical pounding attack that forces the defense to zero in on a narrow focus of plays. That is when these plays really break open. I will talk more about play selection in Chapter 22, but suffice it to say, you never want to be in a position where you have to run a trick play. That's when you look foolish and the defense looks great.

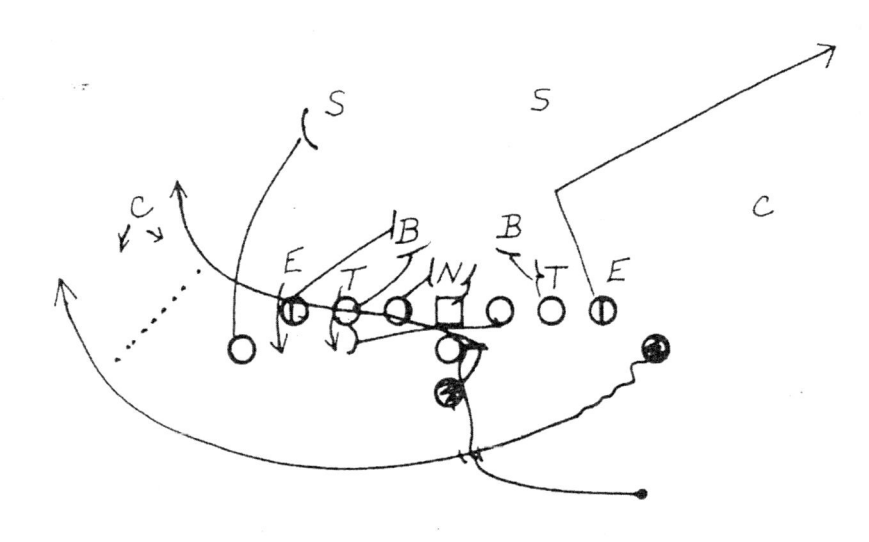

DIAGRAM 7-6 CUT OPTION

POETRY IN MOTION.

Chapter 8

THE PLAY ACTION PASSING SCHEME

All warfare is based on deception.
—Sun Tsu, The Art of War

As I have stated in each chapter, attention to detail must be of utmost concern. Every fake must be carried out to perfection and kept up for ten yards. Every play in the big four except "The Toss" has one to three fakes. These fakes will divide the defense because they must respect each one. As the game goes on, the defense will begin to pay less and less attention to fakes as they figure out the four attack areas of the toss, sweep, cut, and cross toss. It is at this time that the play action game will put the game away for you.

The first rule is never to pass when you think you have to. Never, ever give away an easy turnover. Turnovers will give points away and kill momentum. We have run a cut on a third and 15 situation rather than throw a useless play action where the fakes would be disregarded and the ball easily taken. The ideal time to run any pass play is while your running game is really hot. The defensive backs are sucking up hard to gain enough backup to stop the run, and boom! The play action pass may have to be only an ugly lob that floats from weak-armed quarterback. As long as the defense is thinking run, run, run, they will not cover the pass effectively.

Toss-Pass

Begin with the toss—"pound it until it bleeds." Then run toss-pass (Diagram 8-1). From the off-tight end to the on-tackle, the blocking mode is "aggressive." That is, it's one step forward—two steps back, bluffing a run block to hold the linebackers. The on tight end runs a curl, finding a hole, and sits down in an empty gap in the zone. The onside wing runs a quick corner route, and the fullback runs a flat pattern. The off-wing begins his motion, fakes as if he has received the toss, and blocks the defensive end out and away from the pocket. The quarterback reverses out, fakes the pitch, and pulls the ball back (hiding it on his outside hip) as he completes a half roll, watching the patterns develop. The quarterback should read from deep to short. If the corner has been coming up hard, the wing will be open on a corner route. If the corner hangs deep, but the safety comes up to force, the tight end's curl will be open. When all else fails, the fullback's flat route is always open.

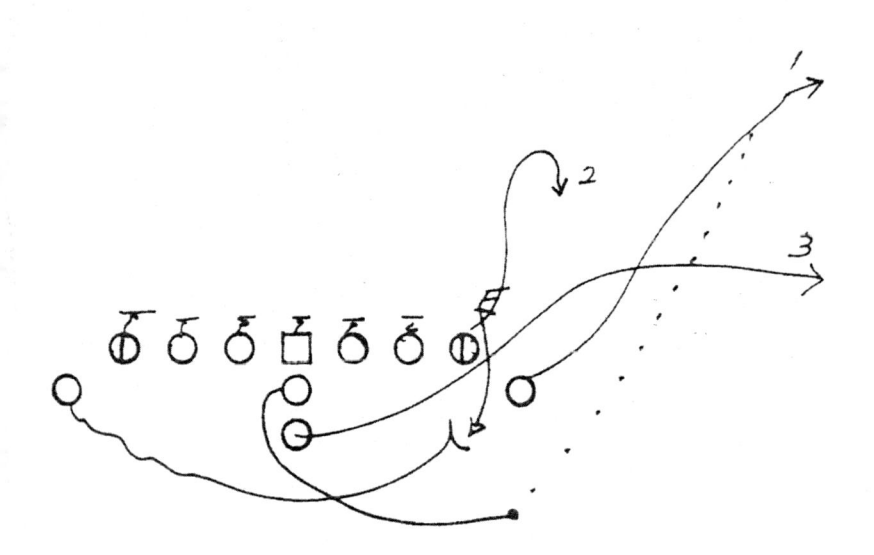

DIAGRAM 8-1 "24 PASS" (TOSS PASS)
Note: O LINE AGGRESSIVE BLOCKS.

Look-In

Another pass off the toss is the look-in pass (Diagram 8-2). This is particularly handy when the defense decides to go into a goal-line set with 10 or 11 men on or near the line of scrim-

The Play Action Passing Scheme

mage. It is also good to use on third and short in keeping with the "pass-when-they-think-run, and run-when-they-think-pass" theory. From the off-tight end to the on-tackle, the blocking mode is "P.P." blocking. P.P. refers to diving forward, aiming your head at your opponent's crotch in order to pull down his hands long enough to allow your quarterback to throw a quick pass. The off-wing runs straight ahead, the motion wing fakes a toss, and the fullback fakes a kick-out block. The onside tight end runs down the seam, but turns his head back over his inside shoulder as soon as he clears the line of scrimmage. He should also have his hands up (pinkies in), creating a pocket that allows the quarterback to see. The tight end should vary his route slightly to get into a clear area fast. The quarterback reverses out with a rotation step toward the toss wing but then plants his foot and rotates back around quickly enough to get set, read the tight end, and make a firm (but not hard) pass. The quarterback's read is simple: If the tight end is open—hit him. If he is covered—throw the ball into the bench. Never force this pass!

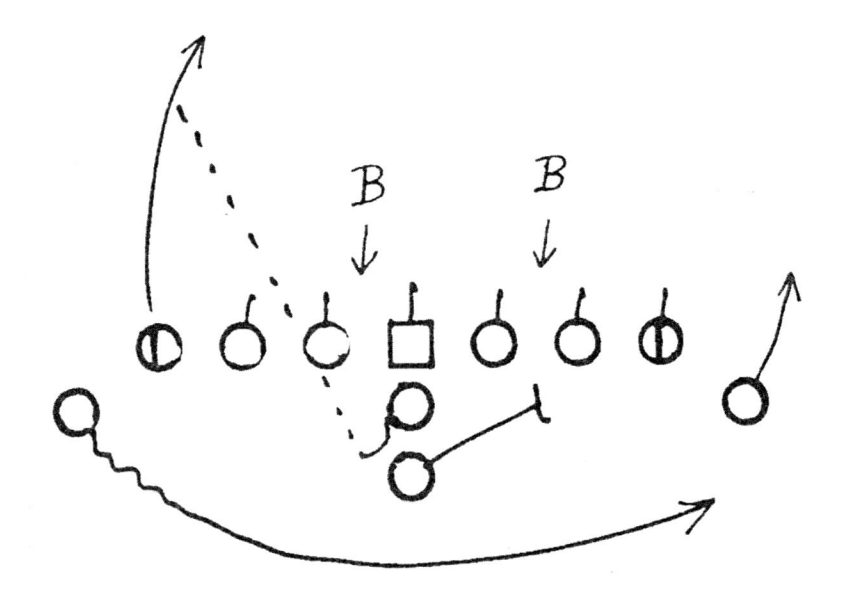

DIAGRAM 8-2 "24 LOOK-IN" (LOOK-IN PASS)

This play works wonders if the tight end is open. The linebackers, in this case, are coming up full speed, while the tight end is going away full speed. The ball may travel only four yards, but the play may gain 30 yards or more. The play is predicated on the aggressiveness of the defense. If the defense wants to stack the line of scrimmage or bring the world on a blitz, run the look-in.

Cross-Toss Pass

The next play will come off the cross-toss action. Let's say you have had great success during the game using the cross-toss. The defense is finally starting to catch up with you by pulling up their safeties and squeezing in their corners to assist in patching the leaky front. You can see this very clearly versus a team that runs a two-deep zone. We would now run our cross-toss pass (Diagram 8-3).

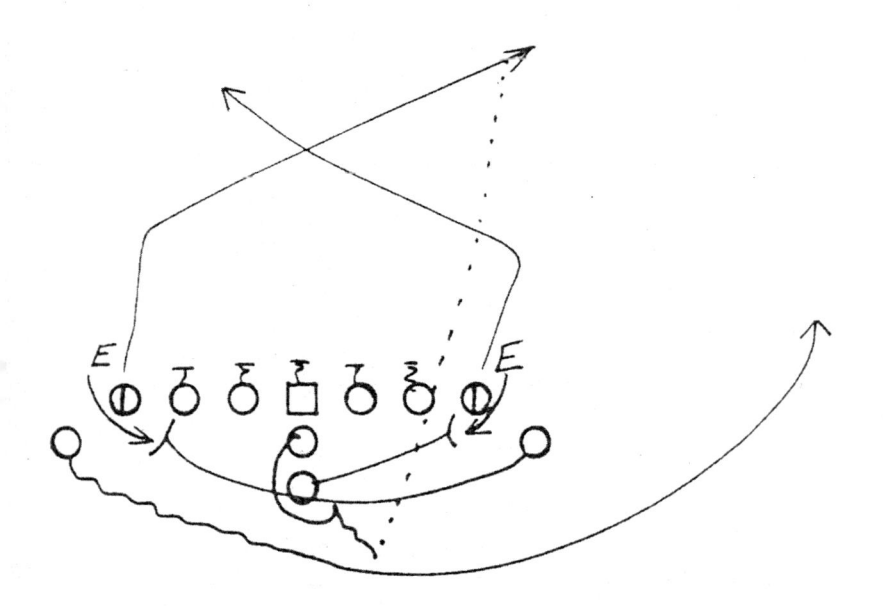

DIAGRAM 8-3 "4 S X-Toss Pass" (X-Toss Pass)

The Play Action Passing Scheme

From tackle to tackle the blocking is aggressive. The motion wing will fake toss action and run down the sideline. The off-wing will come under the quarterback and fake a cross-toss handoff, after which he will block the back side defensive end. The fullback will slip under the cross-toss wing (not colliding with him) and block the front side defensive end. Both tight ends will run a Y-scissors combination, intersecting about 10-12 yards beyond the line of scrimmage. The quarterback will rotate toward the motion wing, fake the toss, finish his rotation to fake the hand-off, then drop back and out (toward the side of his throwing arm because we usually run this only one way) about two-three steps as he chooses which tight end to hit. It is usually easier for him to hit the tight end going away because of the angle. He only needs to loft the ball up over the defenders—who have hopefully sucked up and in—to complete a big gain.

In some ways, this play emulates a flea-flicker, except that it is safer because the ball does not change hands. The quarterback's ball-handling skills and body language will say to the defense, "I don't have it;" he then can pull it out from behind his hip and put six points on the board!

Scissors Pass

To set up the next series of play action, you would run sweep and/or cut until you get the desired results. Remember, every time you run a sweep or cut, the quarterback and tight end carry out a pass (corner route) fake. The quarterback should be observant enough to see if the defensive backs are respecting the fake. As soon as the tight end gets lonely, it is time to run what we call the scissors pass (Diagram 8-4).

The blocking on this play is probably the most complex of any play we run. The back side tackle, guard, and center form a "gate" to seal off the pursuit. Beginning with the center, who rotates back at a 45° angle, the guard and tackle set accordingly, blocking in an inside-out mode. The onside guard pulls, using a deep route. By pulling deep, he allows the onside defensive end to slip inside him. This is on purpose. We want to seal him in and allow the quarterback outside access.

58 Chapter 8

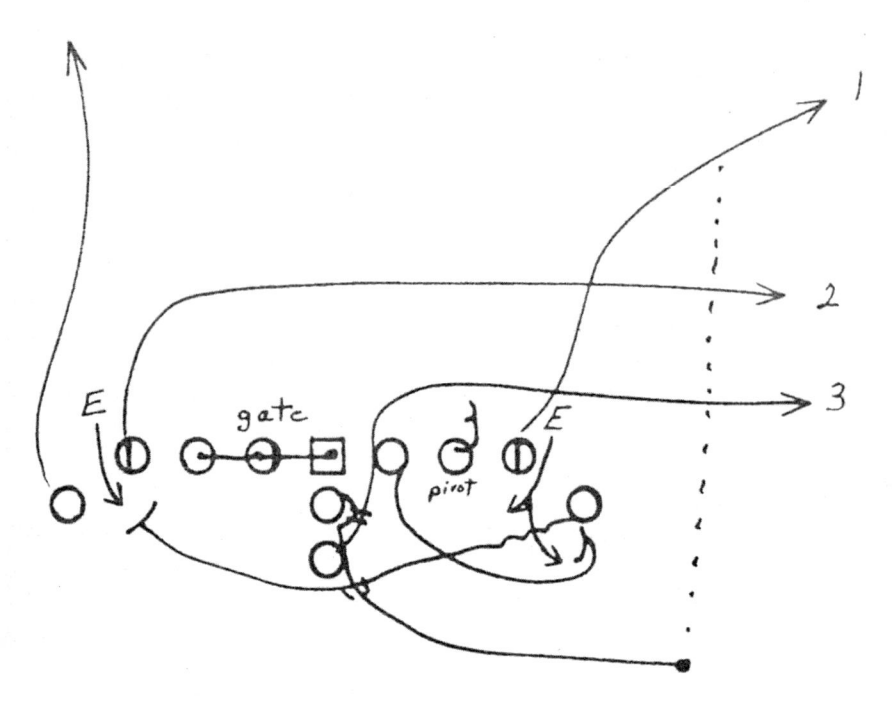

DIAGRAM 8-4 "18 SCISSORS PASS" (SCISSORS PASS)
Note: ONSIDE GUARD SEALS DE

RUNNING TO SET UP THE PASS.

The Play Action Passing Scheme

However, if the defensive end insists on driving deep up field, we will post him and ride him out, using his own momentum. The quarterback must spot this, pull up and set-up in the pocket. The onside tackle will "pivot" block his man, aiming his rear end toward the quarterback's roll, and sealing his man inside. The wing will motion, fake a sweep hand-off, and block the back side defensive end. The off-wing will run a seam route looking back over his inside shoulder. The offside tight end will run a drag in front of the linebacker's drop. The onside tight end runs a corner, looking over his outside shoulder. The fullback will fake a dive through the zero or one hole, then "fill block" for the pulling guard if necessary. If he is not needed, he can continue into a flat route.

The quarterback will fake the fullback handoff, and the sweep handoff, and roll away from the motion. He should first find the pulling guard's rear end to establish where he can set up. As stated before, the defensive end's charge is the determining factor. The ideal situation is to get outside and beyond the mess. The entire blocking scheme is set up to get the quarterback beyond the perimeter and shut the door behind him.

Once the quarterback has rolled free, his vision should be clear. His priorities are again deep to short: First, the onside tight end's corner route; second the off-side tight end's drag; third, the fullback's flat; and finally, if there is time and your quarterback has the skill, he can hit the back side seam. The back side seam is a real killer, and there are times when we will tell the quarterback to look there first, but it takes a strong arm to throw across the field to a receiver who is going away. Another possibility is to have the quarterback take off and run! This creates a whole new problem for the defense, especially the corner back. It is a case of "danged if you do—danged if you don't."

Explode

A few other plays that are really effective in specific settings are explode, bootleg, and pitch pass. The explode is great when used versus goal-line defenses where you get a man-to-man look, and no net (no safety support). With a defense dug in to stop the toss, dive, or sneak, the explode will be open (Diagram 8-5). We once again use the element of surprise afforded us by our monotonous snap count. We go on first sound. The blocking mode from tackle to tackle is P.P. blocking. With the defense reeling in shock, trying to recover and charge forward, we have our wings run quick corners and our tight ends run quick seams—"quick," as in "get over the line of scrimmage and look for the ball!"

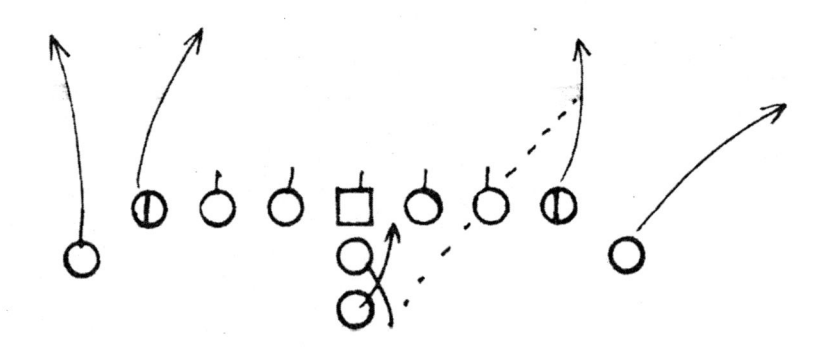

DIAGRAM 8-5 "EXPLODE ON SOUND" (EXPLODE-PASS)
Note: O Line P.P. block

The fullback will dive over the zero hole for window dressing. The quarterback gets the snap, stands as tall as he can, and lofts a pass to the nearest open receiver.

Explode-X

We also run explode-x (Diagram 8-6). It is essential that the quarterback get everybody set for one second, or the play will be called back. This is why we have our offensive line preset in a three-point stance. It is also a good idea to inform the referee of this play, because many times they will be caught sleeping and call the play dead. A slow, lethargic defense that saunters up to the line of scrimmage will pay dearly on this play.

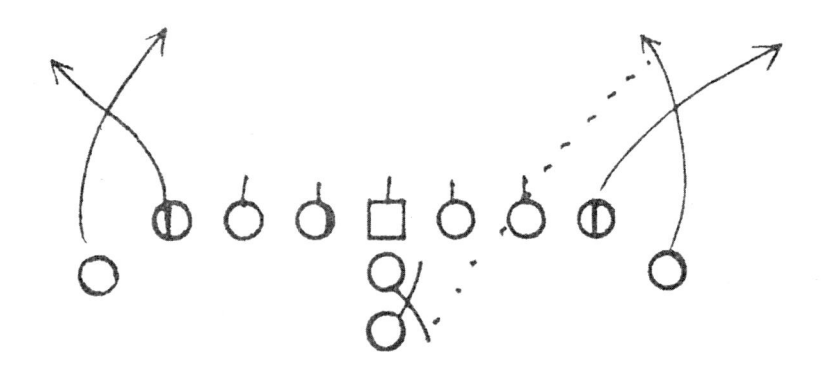

DIAGRAM 8-6 EXPLODE-X PASS

Near Boot

The naked bootleg is useful for a couple of reasons. It is still one of the hardest plays to stop on the goal-line, and it is also very effective versus a defense that is dedicated to reading guards. It uses the two guards as false keys who go the opposite way of the ball. We can actually run this play two ways, depending on the defense's reaction and strength. The first one is a true naked boot we call *near* boot (Diagram 8-7). The word "near" tells the tight end nearest the play call to run a fade. The onside tackle pivots and seals his man inside. The off-guard pulls, sealing the hole created by the onside guard's pull. The center seals his man or covers the guard versus an even. The off-side guard pulls and sets up outside the defensive end. The off-tackle and tight end pivot and seal. The off-wing downblocks the defensive end, forming a double-team with the tight end. The motion wing fakes a sweep. The fullback fakes a dive and should try to run into any leaks in the guard's vacated hole.

The quarterback carries out the scissors progression (fake to fullback, fake sweep) then should roll deep away from the motion. By gaining depth, he will avoid the pursuing defensive end who should be chasing the sweep. (If he reads the boot, the quarterback should pull up early and throw.) If the quarterback gets outside in the clear, he will evaluate the corner read quickly. If the corner has come up, the tight end should break open on the fade. If the corner is hanging back, the quarterback should begin to head upfield, keeping open the option of throwing a quick pass if the corner back changes his mind and tries to attack. The quarterback should stay as close to the sidelines as possible, get as many yards as he can, and either get into the corner of the end zone or out of bounds before taking punishment.

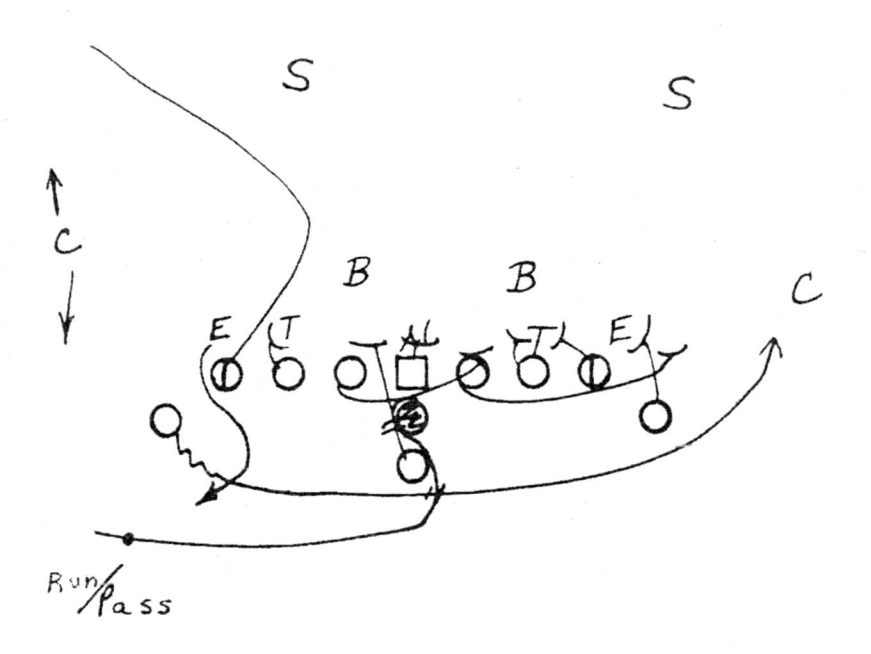

DIAGRAM 8-7   "19 NEAR NAKED BOOTLEG" (NEAR NAKED BOOTLEG)
Note: QB READS CB FOR RUN/PASS READJUSTMENT.

Far Boot

The far naked boot leg changes only in who runs the pattern (Diagram 8-8). The word "far" in this case tells the far tight end to run a sloping drag across the field and the near tight end to "hook block" the defensive end, pinning him inside. This is used if the defensive end is just too good and too smart to be fooled by the boot leg action.

The Play Action Passing Scheme

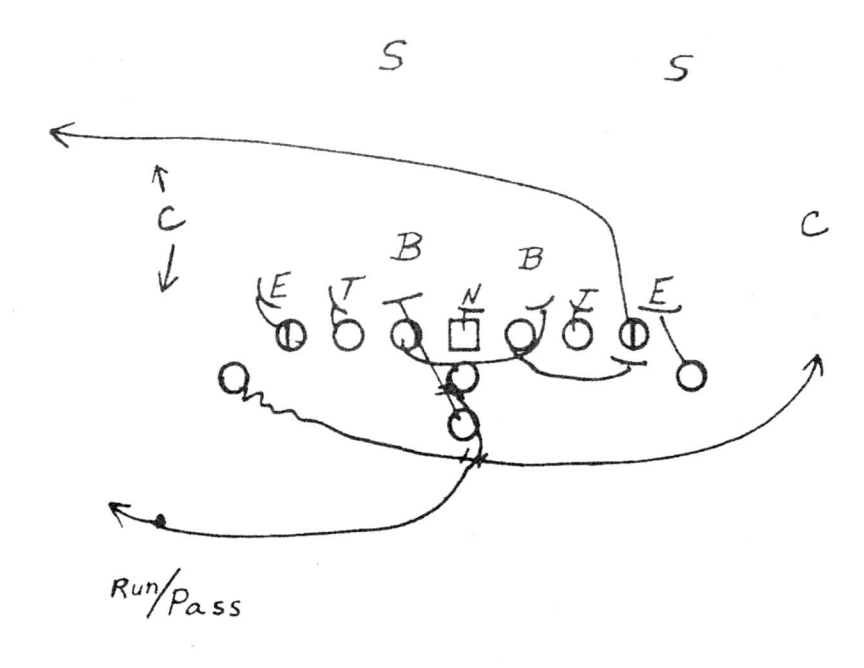

DIAGRAM 8-8 "19 Far Naked Bootleg" (Far Naked Bootleg)

Near or far, this play really complements the offense because it looks exactly like sweep, cut, and an aggressive, well-coached defense that reads will bite hook, line, and sinker.

Pitch Pass

Finally, the old pitch pass remains a deceptive wonder. Visions of Paul Hornung and the Packers once again come to mind. The Packers set it up the way we would: Pound the defense into overreacting, and then throw over the top.

Our pitch pass comes off the toss action. All linemen, including the onside tight end should set an aggressive pivot block to show run, and get into position to seal off their man from the play. The off tight end runs a drag. The onside wing runs a post-corner. He should stutter step as if he were blocking the safety, and then sprint to the corner. The fullback will run a flat pattern after appearing to head out on a kick-out block.

The quarterback reverses out, lobs his toss, and heads toward the would-be toss hole, but then reverses back and catches backside pursuit.

The motion wing gathers in the toss and begins to run, but should arch backwards, losing ground just slightly. As he is running, he should be peeking downfield to see if the other wing's post corner route has broken open. When he gets just about to the area behind the onside tackle, he should pull up, plant his feet and throw. Priority again goes from deep to short, and in the case that everyone is covered, the wing can take off and run.

Play action is the coup de grace to this offense. It cannot be overemphasized that unless the defense has been pounded, and really pounded long enough to begin to overreact, play action is foolish. Never throw when expected to throw. Throw on first down, throw on second and short, but never give easy turnovers by throwing on third and long.

Chapter 9

WINGS ON: COUNTERING LOADED FRONTS

The art of war is simple enough. Find out where your enemy is. Get at him as soon as you can. Strike at him as hard as you can and often as you can, and keep moving on.
—Ulysses S. Grant

When you run the Double Wing, the first thing you will notice is the strange variety of defenses you will see. Sometimes we will see four to five different defensive fronts in one game. What you see most often, though, are the loaded fronts. It is quite common for teams to play with six, seven, even eight men up on the line. This can create problems if they play it properly and have good personnel.

Now, you might automatically be thinking "pass," but that is not the Double Wing mindset. We want to run our game and our game is "Smash Mouth" football. If a team can take us out of what we do best (and what we spend the majority of our practice time on), then they have got us. Instead, we want to out match the overload by putting our wings up on the line, thus creating an overload of our own.

Green: Wing Shifts Up

Our goal is to keep things simple. For instance our play calling is something like, "24 Toss, 24 Toss, ready, break." We know the snap count is always on two, and we know the wing getting the ball will be in motion. We want to keep this simple pattern so when we want our *Wings On*, we simply use two colors: green and black. Green means the wings begin off the line and move up on "Ready." (Our cadence is "Ready, set, hit, hit.") Black means the wings line up on the line of scrimmage, and on "Ready," they move back. The wing who is not going in motion moves up in green (Diagram 9-1). The wing who is going in motion moves back in black (Diagram 9-2).

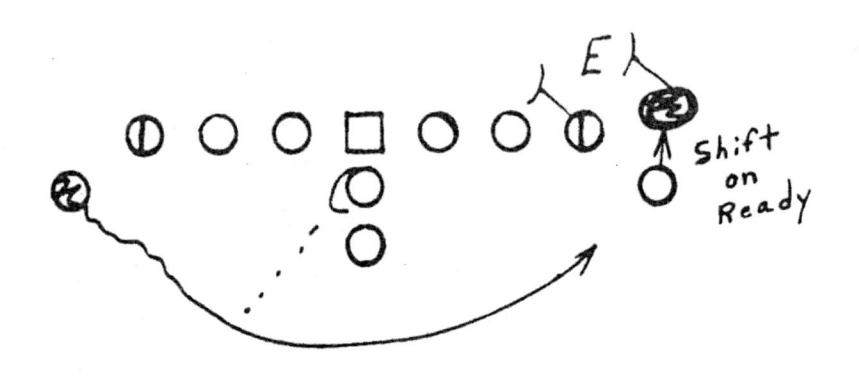

DIAGRAM 9-1 "GREEN 24 TOSS" (GREEN SHIFT)
Note: WING SHIFTS ON "READY."

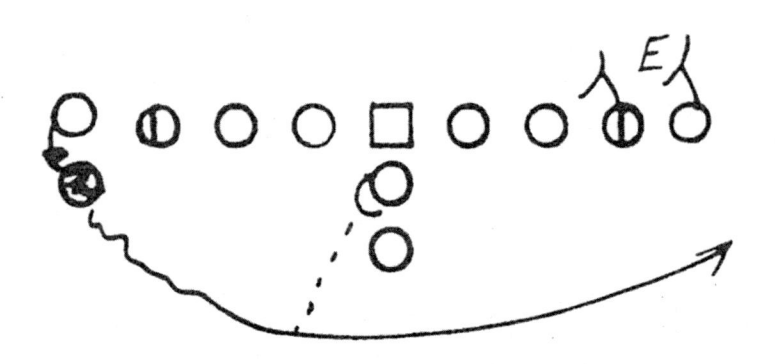

DIAGRAM 9-2 "BLACK 24 TOSS" (BLACK SHIFT)
Note: BOTH WINGS BEGIN "ON."
ON "READY" LEFT WING SHIFTS "OFF."

Wings On: Countering Loaded Fronts

This delayed movement prevents the defense from knowing our set until the last second, thus delaying their adjustments. Remember the rules state that you must have a minimum of seven men on the line; it does not state a maximum. We will run wings on with the Toss, Cross Toss, Sweep, Cut, and more so as not to tip off any plays. And, if we feel we don't need it, we will avoid using it altogether.

Wings On creates big problems for any defense because it spreads the front. It actually creates a larger line of scrimmage with more holes to plug. If the defense reacts, they most likely will employ more defenders to the front, thus thinning their layers (Diagram 9-3). If the defense does not react, they are more susceptible to getting down blocked and walled up at the point of attack.

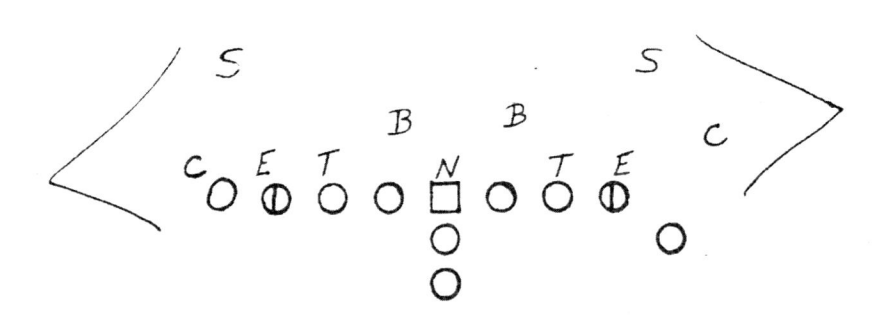

DIAGRAM 9-3   ONE LAYER DEFENSES—7-9 ON L.O.S.

This is when you really can have fun. When you put wings on, it's like adding a 12th and 13th man. You simply out-flank the opponent. The defensive end will have fits trying to figure out where to line up. If he stays inside, he is trapped in the wash. If he slides out beyond the wing, he will create a huge seam inside. For an offensive coordinator there is no greater joy than frustrating the heck out of an opponent.

Black: Wing Shifts Back

Let's look at some basic plays and how we would block them versus loaded fronts. "The Toss" is our key play; without it, we cannot really play *our* game. So if we get a defense who walks up their corners into an okie (5-2), making it a 7-2, we must counter with our wing positioning. Let's say we call "Black, 24 Toss" (Diagram 9-4). The left wing sets back and will get the ball after he begins his motion. The center and right guard double-team the nose. The right tackle and tight end double-team the defensive tackle. The back-side guard and tackle pull as normal. The back-side tight end chops the defensive tackle as usual. The difference comes at the point of attack. The "on" wing now down blocks the defensive end (instead of getting the line-backer) and the fullback now kicks out the corner (instead of the defensive end). What we have done is to simply move the point of attack over one man by matching their overload with our wing.

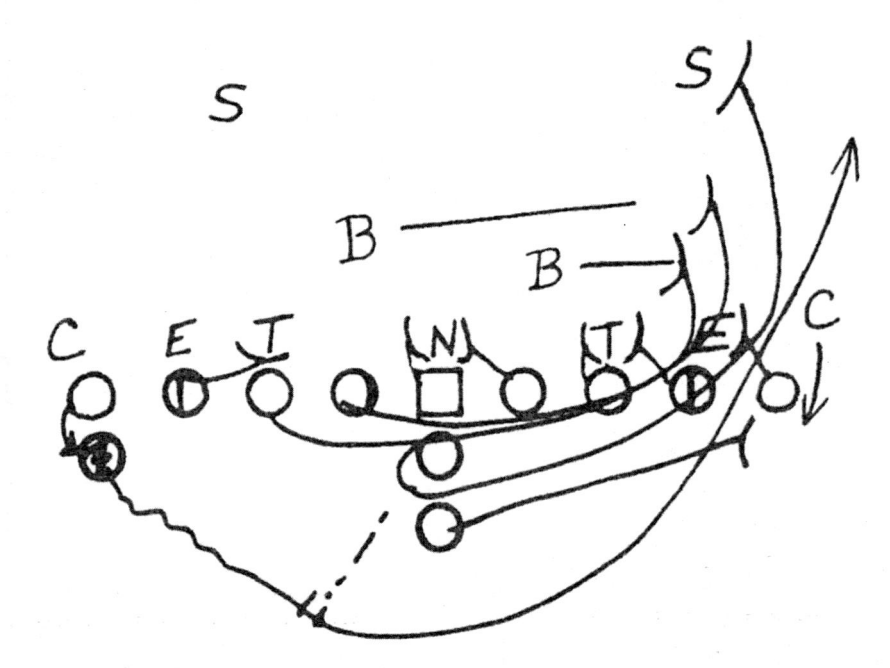

DIAGRAM 9-4   BLACK 24 TOSS VS. 7-2 DEFENSE

A BEAUTIFUL SIGHT—A RUNNER GOING FREE.

Next, we will look at Cross Toss versus a 6-2 defense (Diagram 9-5). This will be a "Green, 24 Cross Toss." Both wings will begin off the line of scrimmage and the left one (the 2-back) will move up on "ready." The right wing (the 4-back) will begin his motion, fake receiving the pitch and carry out a 10-yard fake. The center will call "7-technique" when he sees the even front. He then will seal block the back-side to allow the guard to pull. The onside guard down blocks for the far linebacker. The onside tackle down blocks the man over the guard. The tight end down blocks the man over the tackle. The offside guard continues his pull until he kicks out the defensive end. The offside tackle pulls and turns to seal upfield. The offside tight end chops the defensive tackle; the fullback seals backside pursuit. The quarterback rotates toward the man in motion, faking a pitch. He then pulls the ball back to his hip, continues to rotate 360° and gives an inside handoff to the 2-back. By running this play, we can stop the defense from keying on the overloaded side because we go away from the on wings side.

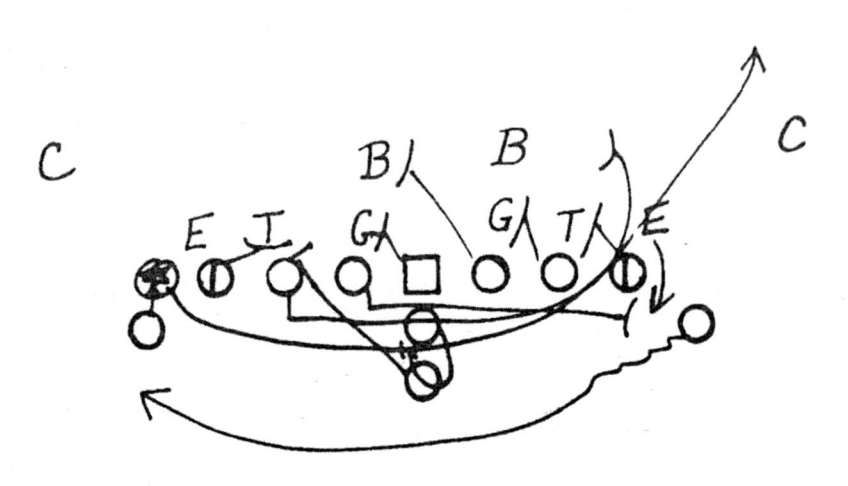

DIAGRAM 9-5 GREEN 24 X-TOSS VS. 6-2 DEFENSE

If we want to go outside, we will call a sweep; for example, "Black, 28 Sweep" versus a 6-2 with corners up making it an 8-2 defense (Diagram 9-6). As crazy as it may seem, we have seen this defense several times in the middle of the field. Both wings will begin on and the 2-back will set back on "Ready." He will begin his motion and receive the ball. The center will again call "Seven" unless previously decided on by our scouting report. He will seal block the back-side.

The onside guard will pull shallow and wide as possible. His goal is to get beyond the corner back (now responsible for containment) and trap him inside. If he cannot trap his man because of the corner's attack, then he must either drive him or center punch him in the chest to give the runner a chance to cut inside or out race him to the corner. The onside tackle down blocks the man over the guard. The tight end down blocks the man over tackle. The wing down blocks the defensive end. The back-side guard pulls and cleans up the tunnel, or gets through and turns up to attack first man down field. The tight end runs a corner route as a decoy. The fullback fakes a dive. The quarterback fakes the dive, gives the sweep and carries out a fake roll and throw.

Wings On: Countering Loaded Fronts

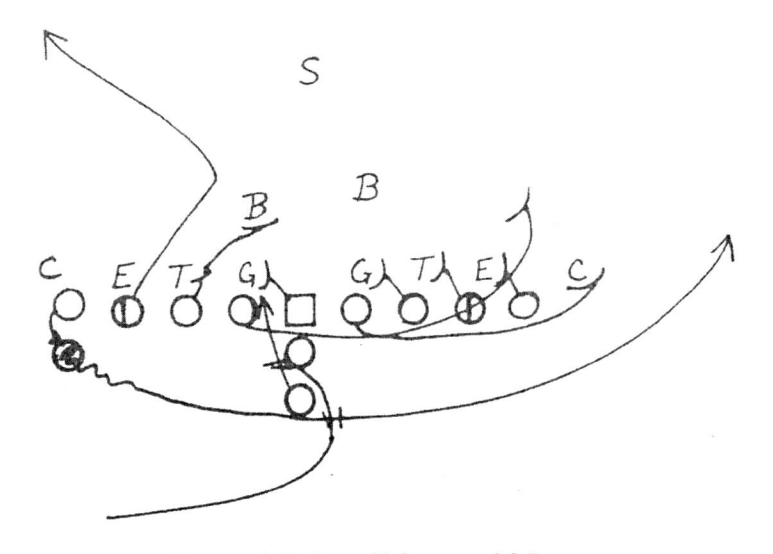

DIAGRAM 9-6   BLACK 28 SWEEP VS. 8-2 DEFENSE

If the defense is beginning to react to the Wings On, a great play to call is the Cut; for instance, "Black, 30 Cut" versus a 7-2, okie with corners up (Diagram 9-7). With both wings *on*, the 2-back shifts off, then motions. The right side is overloaded so if the corner isn't up yet, he will begin to crowd up to match the unbalanced set. What this creates is one layer and limited back up (two linebackers in the middle, and two safeties deep). So if the fullback pops free of the line of scrimmage, he can go unhindered for big yards. The center and *on* guard double the nose, the tackle and *on* tight end loop around the defensive tackle (the trap man) and double the linebacker. The *on* wing releases to block the safety. The off guard pulls to either trap the defensive tackle if he is shallow, or lead block downfield. The off tackle seals and releases. The off tight end runs a corner route. The quarterback gives to the fullback, fakes sweep and fakes a roll and throw. The fullback takes the inside handoff and cuts right behind the guard and aims for the corner. This play is devastating versus a single-layer defense.

These plays and more can be enhanced by the wing overload. It is a way in which you can equalize an opponent's attempt to "stack the deck" and stop your best plays. This does

72   *Chapter 9*

not mean we will never pass, especially if the defense is vulnerable, but we don't want to have our opponent dictate what we run. The Wings On is also a great way to gain an edge on any normal defense by quickly creating an unbalanced situation.

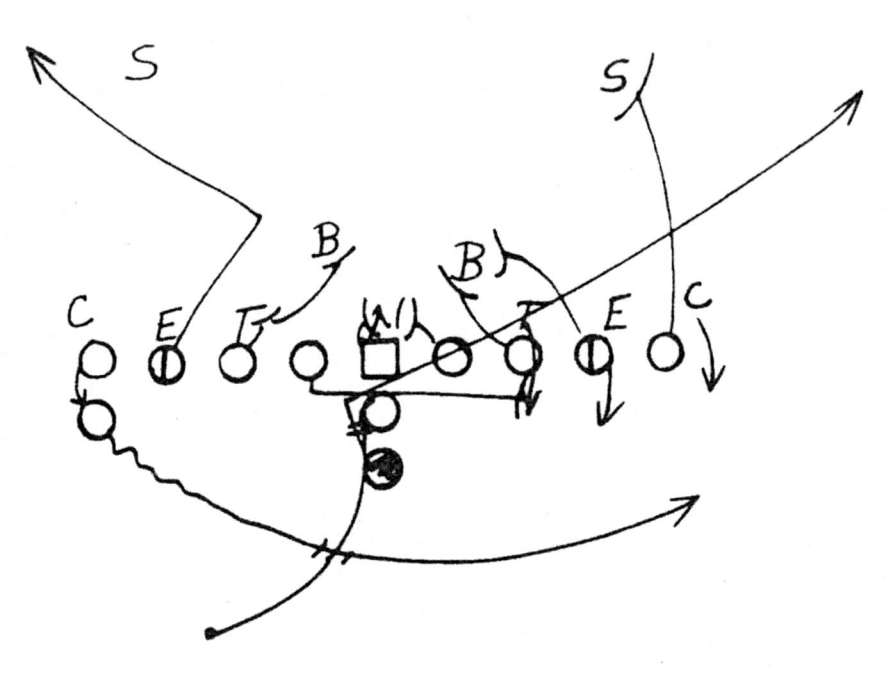

DIAGRAM 9-7   BLACK 30 CUT VS. 7-2 DEFENSE

Chapter 10

Double-Team Schemes for "The Toss"

*In life, as in a football game, the principle to follow is:
Hit the line hard.*
—Theodore Roosevelt

In a previous chapter, I explained our two possible blocking modes, Base and Seven: Base being our double-teaming mode versus odd fronts, and Seven being our pattern versus stunting, slanting, or even fronts. After listening to Don Markham's clinic, I am convinced that it is possible to utilize double-teams against any front when running "The Toss" play.

Versus 5-2

We will begin with attacking a basic 5-2 defense. However, it is important to note that we rarely see this used against us anymore. Teams prefer to bring much more man power to the front, as in 6-2 or 7-1. We will look at all of these as well. Versus the 5-2 our center will post, and the on-guard will drive to double the nose. The tackle and the onside right end will double the defensive tackle. The wing will loop the defensive end and seal the onside linebacker. The off-guard and tackle will pull and the off tight end will chop the defensive tackle. The two double-teams will drive the defensive linemen back and down—so much so that they usually catch the linebackers and sometimes defensive backs in the wash, thus cutting off their pursuit (Diagram 10-1).

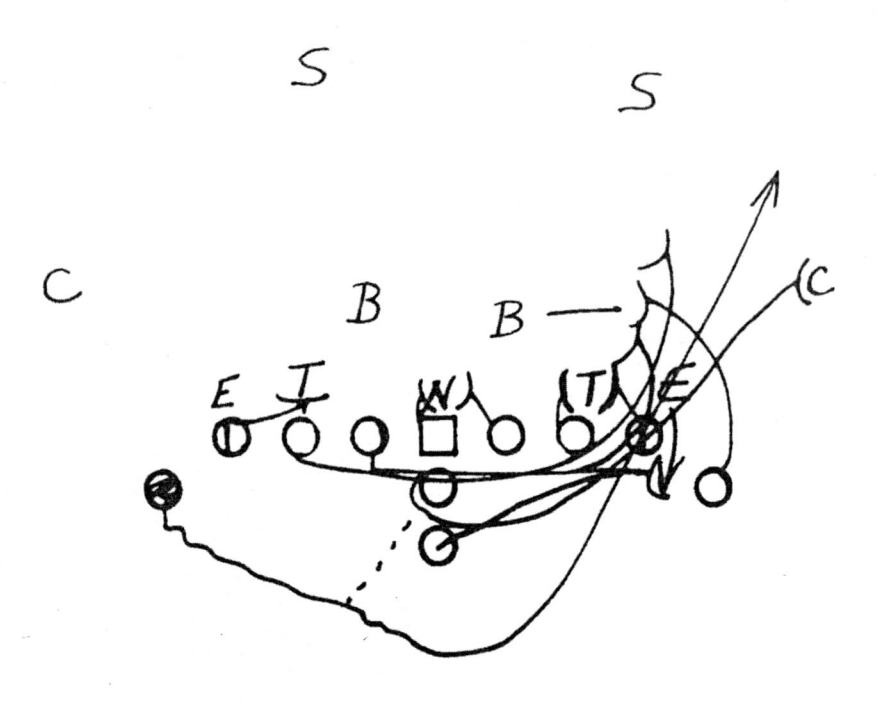

DIAGRAM 10-1   24 TOSS VS. 5-2 DEFENSE

Versus 7-2

Next we will look at attacking a 7-2 defense. That's a 5-2 with the corners up on the line of scrimmage. We would bring our wings up (Chapter 9), but let's look at a couple of ways to play it without altering our basic formation. The first way would be to down block the defensive end without using our wing and keep the two double-teams (nose and defensive tackle). We would then treat the corner back like the defensive end and kick him out with our fullback (Diagram 10-2). Another way to attack this same defense is to block it just like a 5-2, but have the quarterback (who is responsible for the corner back anyway) go after the corner back with a shallow inside-out blocking angle similar to the fullback. This will allow the play to run up and under both the defensive and corner back. Many times these guys penetrate so deep anyway, they take themselves out of the play without even being blocked (Diagram 10-3).

DOUBLE-TEAM SCHEMES FOR "THE TOSS" 75

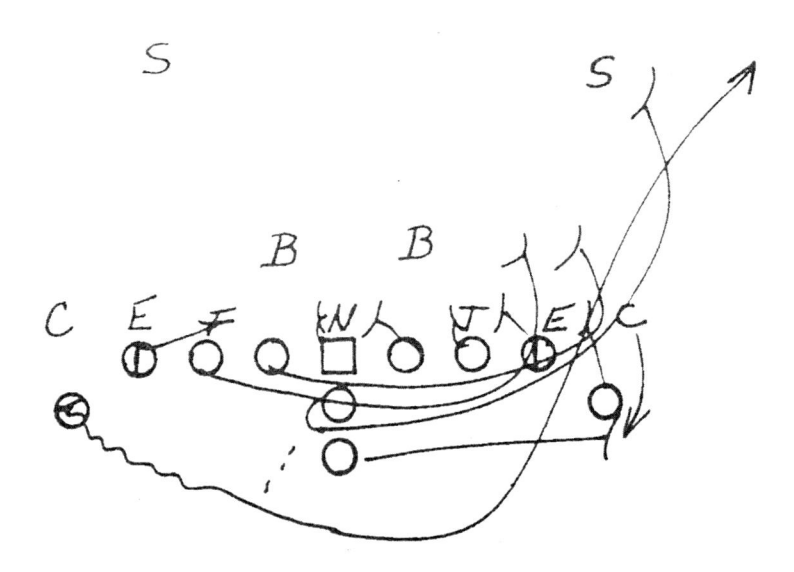

DIAGRAM 10-2 24 TOSS VS. 7-2 DEFENSE

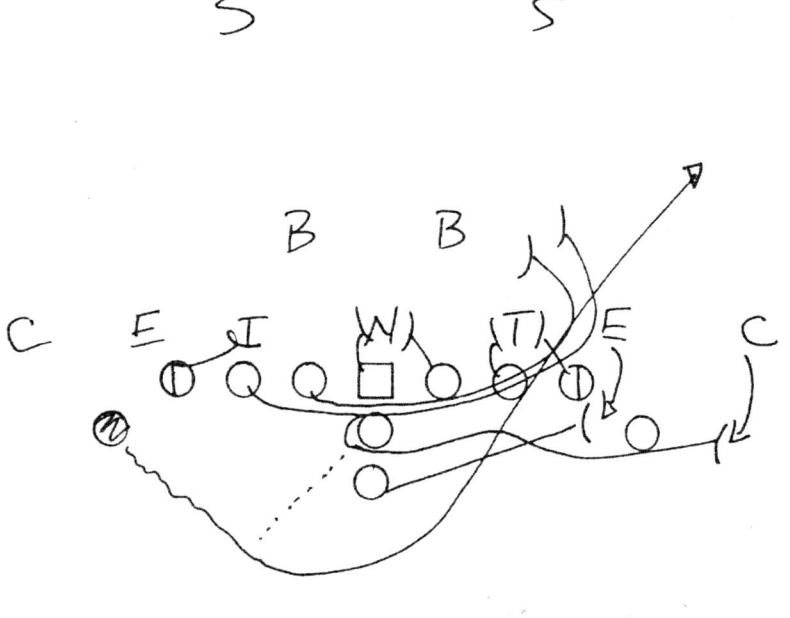

DIAGRAM 10-3 24 TOSS VS. 7-2 DEFENSE NORMAL DEs

Versus 6-2

Next we will take on a 6-2 defensive. Although it might be better to use the Wings On scheme, we can still run this from our normal offensive set-up as well. The center will seal the backside. We will double the defensive guard using our guard and tackle. We will double the defensive tackle with our tight end and wing. We will kick out the defensive end as effectively as usual. The only thing we lack is a linebacker seal block with the onside wing. This will be taken care of by our pulling guard and tackle. Remember, if you get the surge you should, the double-teams will drive their men right into the pursuit path of the linebackers anyway (Diagram 10-4).

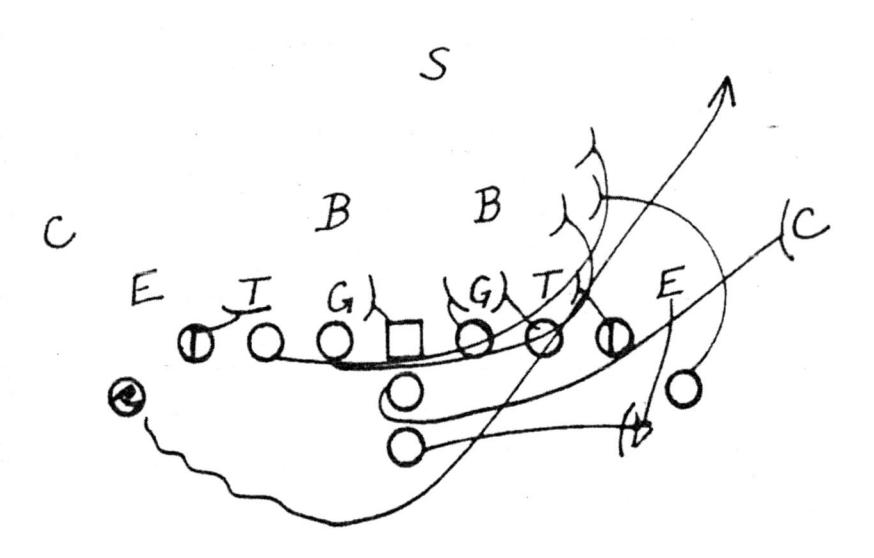

DIAGRAM 10-4   24 TOSS VS. 6-2 DEFENSE
Note: DBL TEAM DG

Versus 7-1

The 7-1 is commonly used against the double wing. We can at least get one double-team here, but to do it we must use Wings On. The center blocks back-side. The onside guard blocks the nose. The onside tackle blocks the defensive guard. The tight end will set the post block for the double-team versus the defensive tackle. Now the tight end might have to really dig down the line because the tackle may be one man away. The wing (now on the line of scrimmage) will join the double and drive the defensive tackle back and down into the linebacker. We will then kick-out the defensive end and the quarterback gets the corner back (Diagram 10-5).

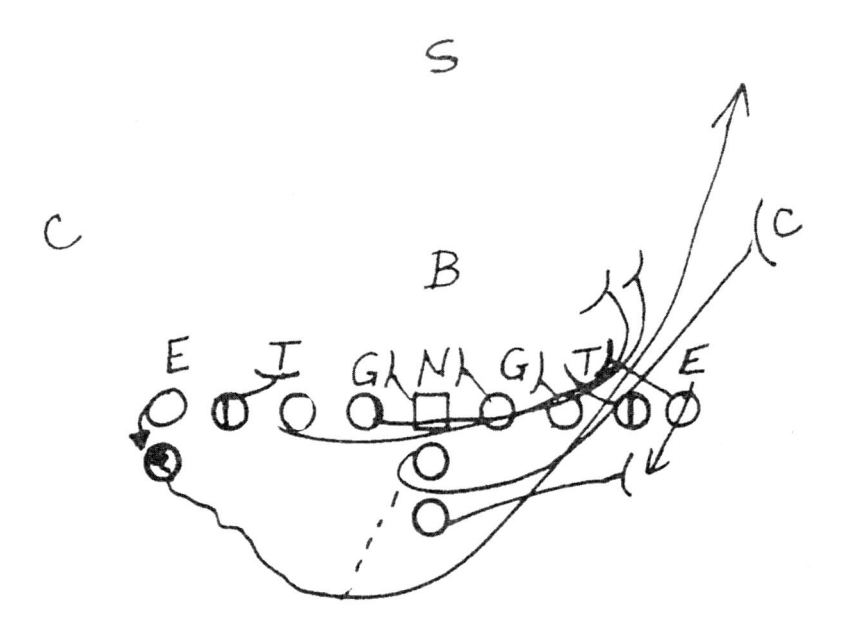

DIAGRAM 10-5 BLACK 24 TOSS VS. 7-1 DEFENSE
Note: DBL TEAM DT

Versus 6-5

Many teams use a 6-5 goal-line stance, and the blocking scheme for "The Toss" can go a couple of different ways depending on what the defensive end plans to do. A coaching note on goal-line play calling: Since the amount of space really shrinks in the red zone (inside the 20-yard line) and teams seem to naturally bunch up inside, the sweep becomes an excellent play especially to the field side. But "The Toss" can and does work fine. To block a 6-5 with defensive ends who are a shade outside of our tight ends, we would double-team the defensive tackle, kick-out the defensive end, and search and destroy the corner back (even if the corner back is on the line of scrimmage) with our quarterback (Diagram 10-6). If the defensive end is inside our tight end, we would use Wings On and double-team him. We then would kick-out the corner back (or possibly the outside linebacker if he has containment responsibility) (Diagram 10-7).

There are obviously more defensive fronts that may be used against "The Toss," but the ones I've covered are the most commonly used against the double wing. By using our original "Base" technique, we can double-team basic odd fronts. By using the "Seven" technique, you can have a simple (easy to remember) attack versus basic even fronts. But by adding these double-team schemes to your game plan, you can continue to create mismatches against any front you may encounter. By striving to include the double-teams, you ensure yourself the walling off effect needed to run "The Toss" consistently.

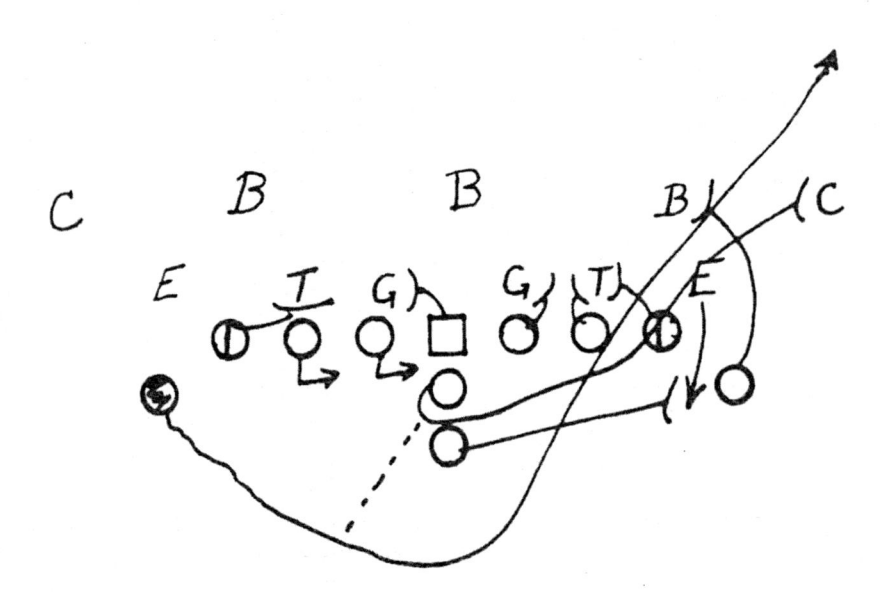

DIAGRAM 10-6 24 TOSS VS. 6-5 (NORMAL DE)

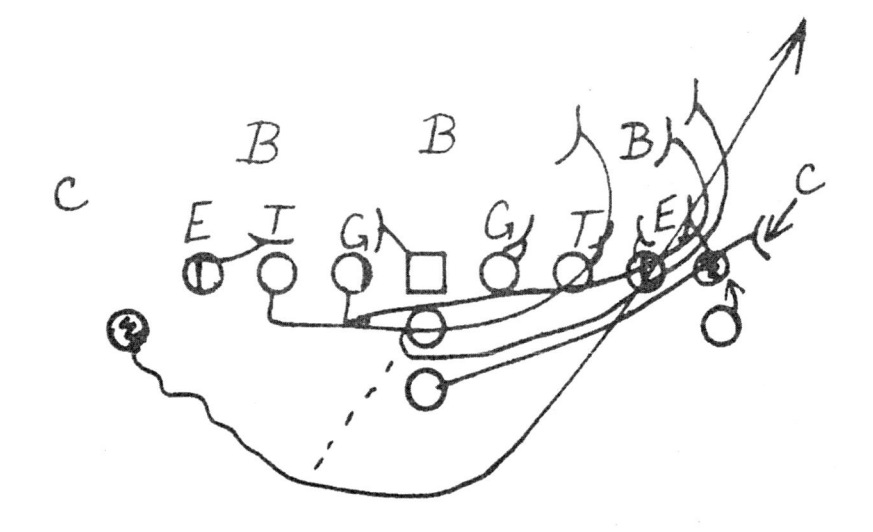

DIAGRAM 10-7 GREEN 24 TOSS VS. 6-5 (DEs INSIDE)

OVERLOAD AT THE POINT OF ATTACK.

Part Four
Changing the Look, Keeping the Concept

Variations & Strategies

Chapter 11

Advanced Double Wing Running Plays

Take calculated risks.
—George S. Patton

After meeting with Coach Markham during one summer, we decided to install some more of his inspired genius into our offense. These plays account for a large portion of our scores.

Quarterback Blast

The first play we installed was a quarterback blast. The play puts one more weapon into our mix. We feel we spread the defense's attention by utilizing both wings and a fullback. Now throw in the quarterback blast, and you simply have too many men to cover consistently. On our "10 Blast" versus a 5-2 defense (Diagram 11-1), we would double the nose with our center and onside guard. We will single seal block the defensive tackles with our tackles. We will get the safeties with our tight ends. The motion wing will decoy sweep action while the onside wing will go and block a corner. The off guard will aim to put a down-field seal on his linebacker. The fullback will take an inside out aim at the other linebacker. The quarterback takes the snap, rotates toward the motion, fakes sweep action, pulls the ball back, continues his 360° turn and follows the fullback through the hole.

The results are amazing if you have already pounded the defense with the wings or the fullback. The beautiful part of it is that the defense won't see that the quarterback has the ball until he has broken past the linebackers. There are only a few changes versus a 6-2 even front (Diagram 11-2).

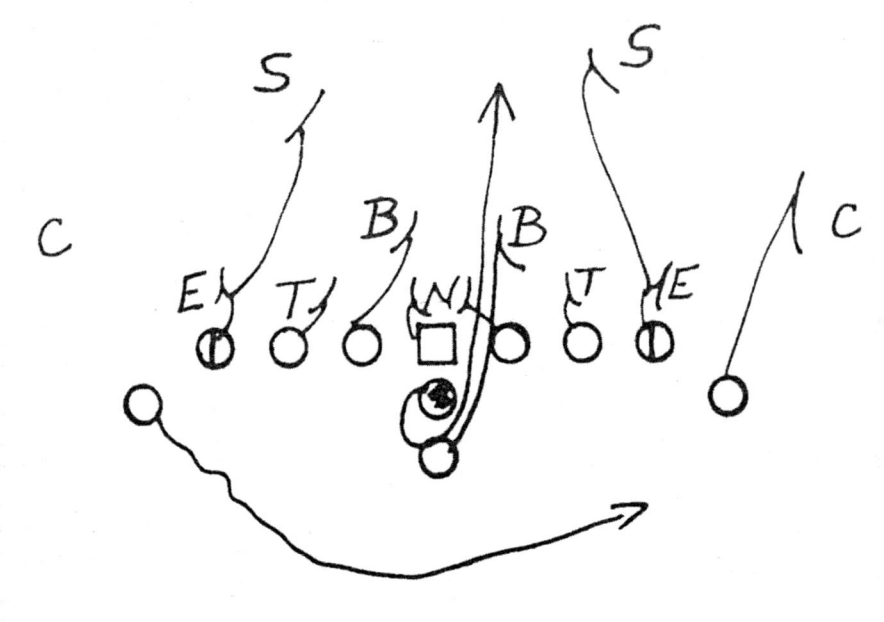

DIAGRAM 11-1 10 BLAST VS. 5-2

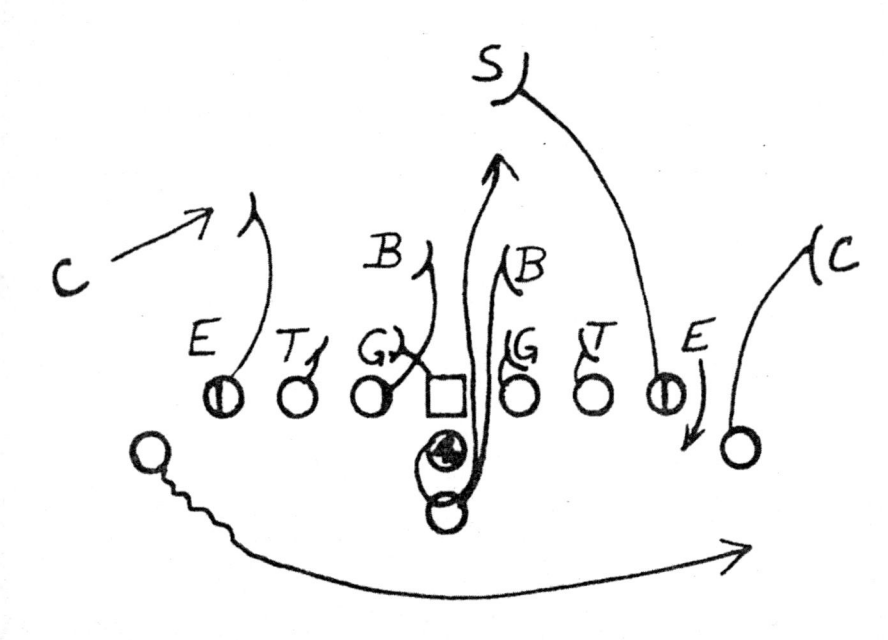

DIAGRAM 11-2 10 BLAST VS. 6-2

Reverse

Another play we borrowed from Markham is what we call "reverse." This is a counter to the sweep. In our "24 Reverse" (Diagram 11-3), we begin what looks like a 49 Sweep with the left wing in motion. The center and onside guard double the nose. The tackle and onside tight end double the defensive tackle. The off guard pulls and kicks out the defensive end. The offside tackle pulls and will be joined in his travels by the fullback (who has first taken a false step toward the motion). These two travel in tandem; then the tackle turns up and in to seal the inside, and the fullback turns up and out to seal the outside. The back-side tight end chops the defensive tackle. The quarterback turns toward the motion wing and hands him the ball. The quarterback then can double back, trailing the wing who is carrying the ball, as an option pitch man, or if he is too slow to be a run threat, can simply help lead block. The 2-back comes past the 4-back, receives the ball and follows the train of blockers to daylight.

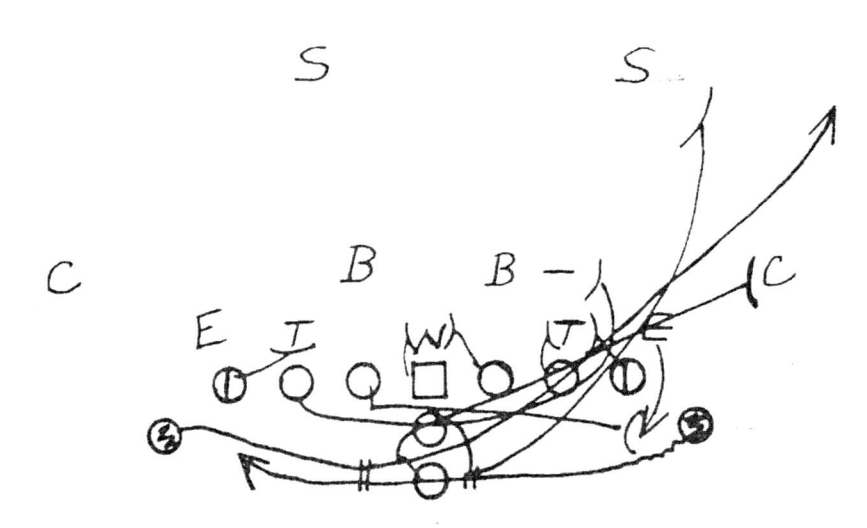

DIAGRAM 11-3 24 REVERSE VS. 5-2

Keeper

Another play you can use as a counter to the sweep is the "Quarterback Keep." On a "19 Keeper" versus a 5-2, the 2-back starts his motion and continues to fake sweep action. The fullback fakes dive action. If a defense is reading the backfield's flow, they will be flying to stop the sweep, especially if you have noticed the back-side abandoning caution in an effort to get to the ball. The center base blocks the nose, putting his head on the play-side gap. The offside tackle and tight end do the same with their men. The onside tight end down blocks the defensive tackle. We will pull the onside tackle and guard as well as the offside guard. The tackle will hook the defensive end. The on guard will get the corner back. The off guard will get first threat after that. The off wing will block down field. The quarterback rotates toward the motion, gives the sweep fake, hides the ball on his hip and rolls away. Once he feels the blocking has had time to set up, he will change speed and head upfield (Diagram 11-4).

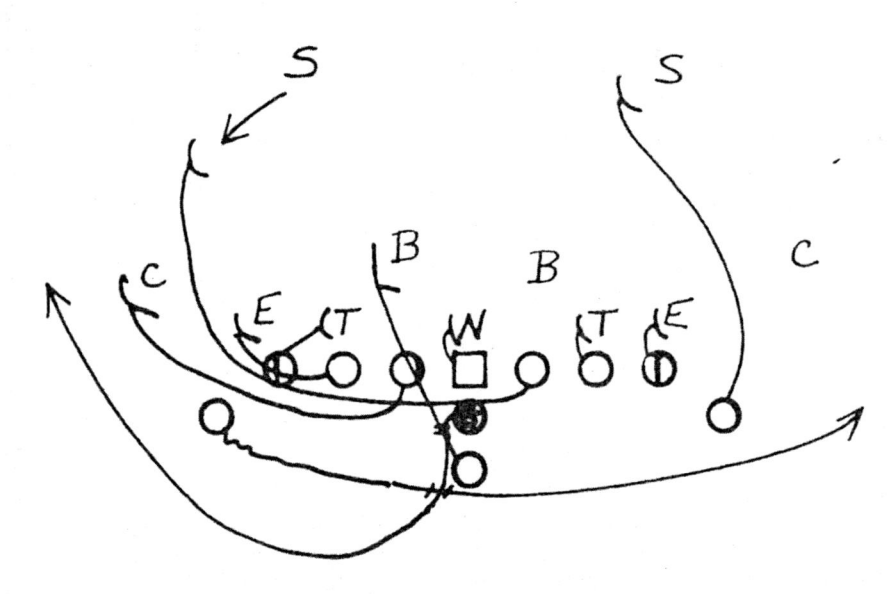

Diagram 11-4 19 Keeper vs. 5-2

ADVANCED DOUBLE WING RUNNING PLAYS

Dive-Cross-Toss Fake

Even the simple dive can be made more deceptive with the double wing. We run ours with wedge blocking (Diagram 11-5). The deception comes by carrying out reverse action after the quarterback gives the dive. The linebacker's eyes will focus on the wings' action while the fullback slips by him.

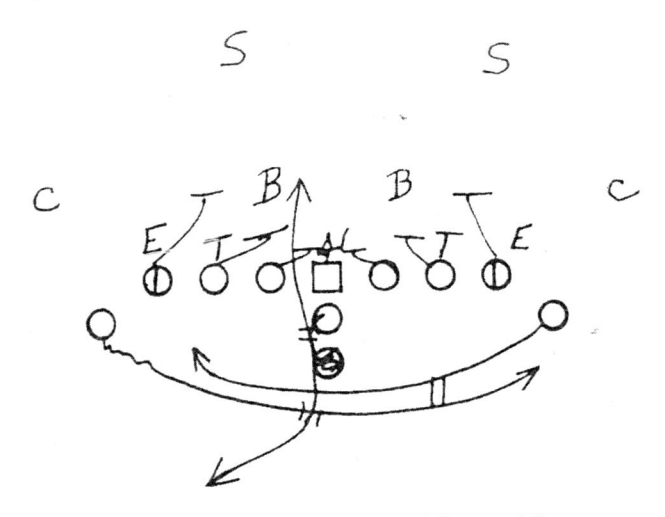

DIAGRAM 11-5   31 (FAKE REVERSE) DIVE VS. 5-2

Phil Bravo of Centaurus High School came up with this. He even bet his starting linebackers a burger if they could identify the ball carrier the first time he ran it. Needless to say he did not lose any money.

Toss Sweep

Another play Phil has given us is a pitch-sweep. We have found that teams who really scouted us began reading the arc of our wings' motion. If it was deep they yelled, "Toss." If it was shallow, they would call out "Sweep" or "Trap." The pitch sweep destroys that tendency key and also gives you more blockers at the point of attack. The wing shows a deep Toss motion. The fullback leads. The quarterback rotates toward motion and pitches the ball. So far all of these actions show Toss. However, the on wing hooks the defensive end. The tight end downs the defensive tackle. The tackle downs the linebacker. The center seals the nose. Both guards pull as normal. The back-side tackle and tight end go down field. Now the ball carrier has two guards as well as the fullback and quarterback to lead block—Look out Vince Lombardi! (Diagram 11-6).

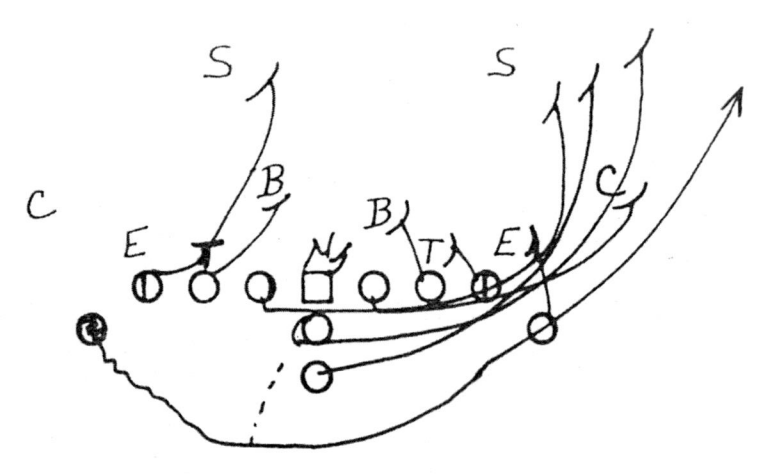

Diagram 11-6 28 Pitch Sweep vs. 5-2

An example of outflanking your opponent.

Advanced Double Wing Running Plays   89

Toss Keep

A play we developed in mid-season was our 14 and 15 Toss. Toss is really a misnomer because the ball stays with the quarterback. We developed this because of our quarterback's ability to run and to set up a pass play off the same action. The play is exactly like the regular Toss (Diagram 11-7), but the wing fakes and goes wider to draw out the corner back, and the quarterback keeps the ball, following the fullback through the hole.

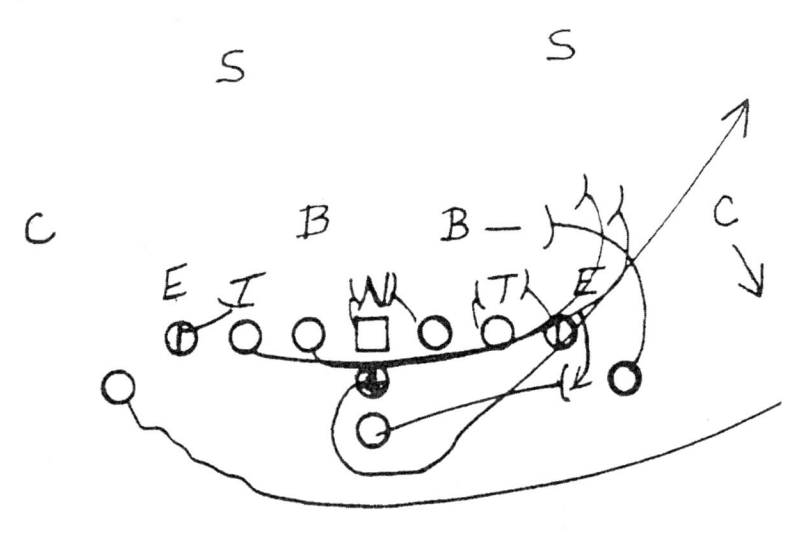

Diagram 11-7   14 Toss vs. 5-2

Guard Trap

Now for some fun. You have a guard who has worked hard all year and you want to throw him a bone. Here's a Markham special you will enjoy. The play is run exactly like a cut except that the fullback traps (kicks out) the defensive tackle and the guard gets to run. The rules state that an offensive lineman must turn and face away from the line of scrimmage (90°) and be one yard deep in the backfield in order to receive the ball legally. So the guard must pivot, plant, raise his upfield elbow and receive the ball. The quarterback takes the snap, takes one step back, then makes the handoff to the guard. Believe it or not you can gain big yards on this one too, depending on your guards (Diagram 11-8).

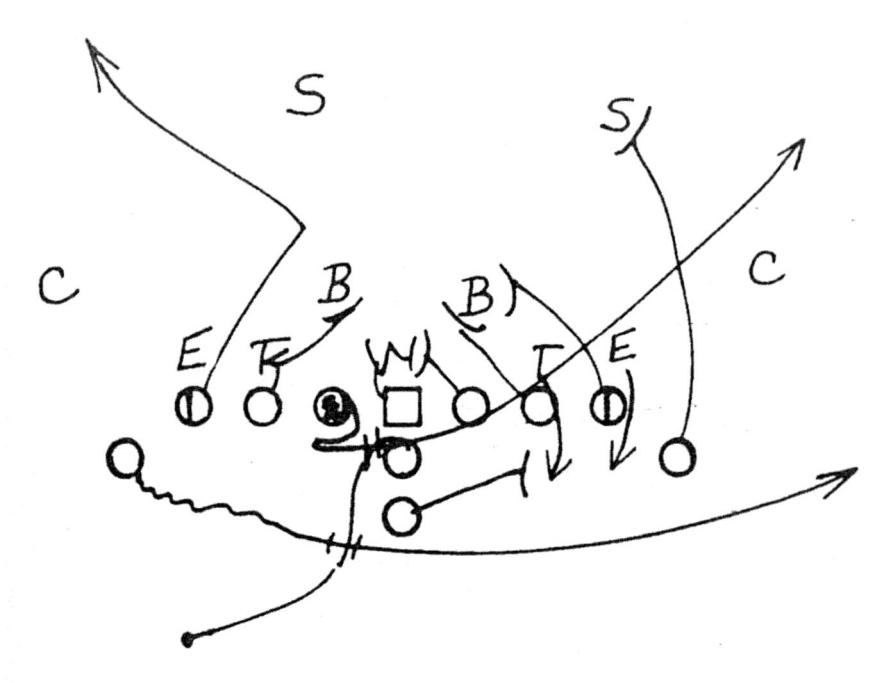

DIAGRAM 11-8   GUARD TRAP RIGHT VS. 5-2

Yo-Yo Toss

Along the line of No Play-plays, we have two more for defenses who enjoy celebrating the fact that they did not jump offside. The first is what we call "Yo-Yo, Motion, Toss." For instance, the 2-back starts his motion to the right (like in 24 Toss), goes past the fullback, and goes all the way to the point behind the offside tackle. He then reverses back still in a deep arching pattern, receives the pitch, and we run 25 Toss (Diagram 11-9). The cadence would be, "Ready, set, hit, hit,...hit, hit." By the fourth "hit," the wing should be coming back toward the play side. It takes timing, but the results are that the defense has jumped offside or has abstained and is celebrating. At this point, it is too late because before they can reset themselves we have begun our charge!

ADVANCED DOUBLE WING RUNNING PLAYS

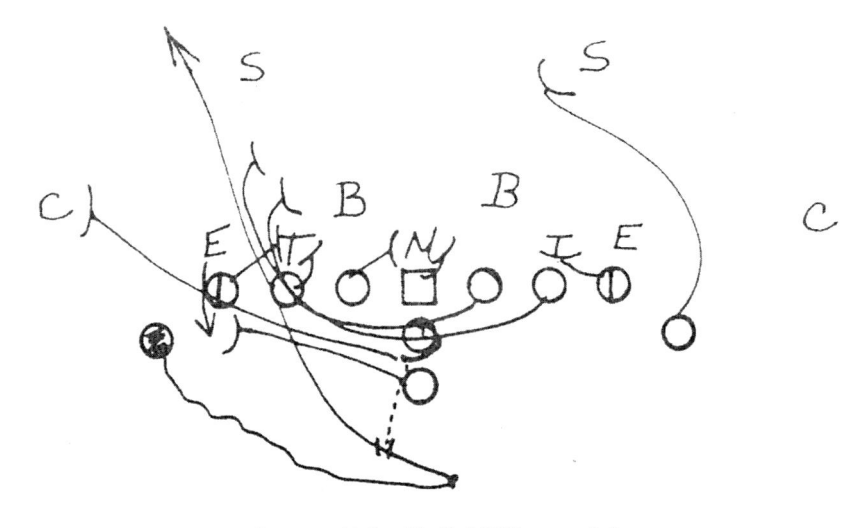

DIAGRAM 11-9 "YO-YO" 25 TOSS VS. 5-2

Wing to I Toss

Another way to rig the same type of play is to have your wing come back to the I-tailback position and stop. He should be about 10 yards deep. From there the quarterback calls "set" right before the next "hit." This tells everyone when the ball will be snapped for the I-Toss. The complete cadence would be "Ready, set, hit, hit, hit, hit." (By now the defense assumes that you are not going to run a play because they have scouted you and know you always go on two.) The quarterback will then bark out, "set" a second time and then, "hit." The same results should occur (Diagram 11-10); that is, you will have a relaxed defense thinking that you're not going to run. More I-formation technique is discussed in Chapter 13.

These new plays should add a few more arrows to your quiver, but don't forget that the double wing philosophy is to work a few plays to perfection. Every time you add a new play to your arsenal, you reduce the time you spend on the rest. These are meant to enhance the basic plays in certain situations. And, of course, different plays fit different personnel. If one clicks for you, then use it as a regular weapon, but don't get spread too thin.

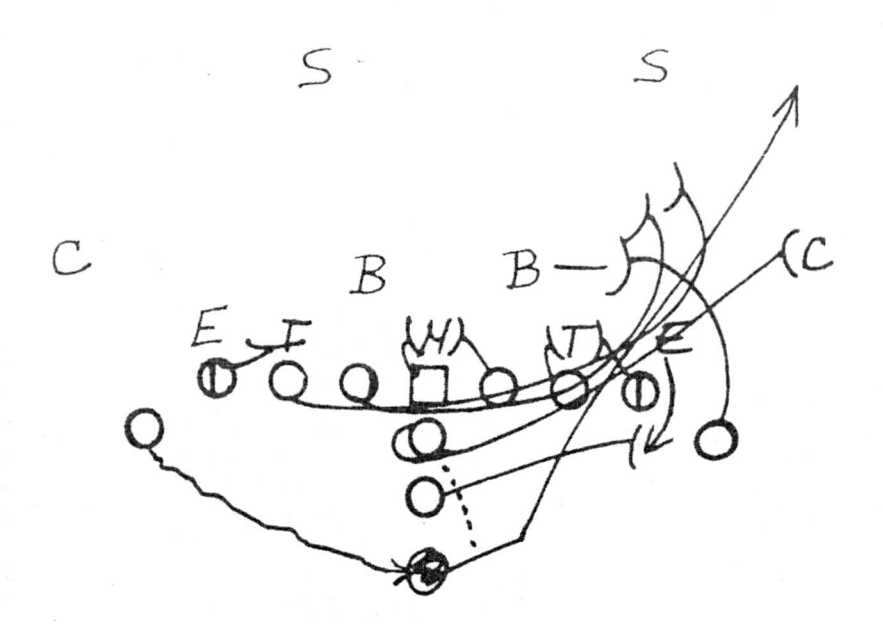

DIAGRAM 11-10 MOTION TO "I"—24 TOSS VS. 5-2

Chapter 12

ADVANCED DOUBLE WING PASSING PLAYS

*Arts long hazard, where no man may choose
whether he play to win or toil to lose.*
—Edwin A. Robinson

The passing game is a small part of the double wing attack, but that does not mean it is ineffective or inefficient. Once you establish the powerful running game that forces the defense to overplay the run, because of mis-matches at the point of attack, they open up big holes for potential big passing gains.

Toss Keep Pass

The 14 and 15 Toss mentioned in the previous chapter forces the defense to attack up hard or be blown away. We have had sources tell us that they are keying on our wings' block. The defensive corners are taught to read the wings' action. If the wing blocks down, the corner must come up to help support the run. So if we run 24 Toss or 14 Toss, and the corner is crashing, and then run "14 Toss Pass" (Diagram 12-1), it's all over but the crying! The wing fakes a down block on the defensive end and then slips behind the corner back. The quarterback fakes run action with his eye on the corner back. If the bluff works, he can lob (even on the run) a four-yard pass for an 80-yard gain. If the corner backs stay back, the quarterback keeps the ball and runs.

94   Chapter 12

SEARCHING FOR AN OPEN RECEIVER.

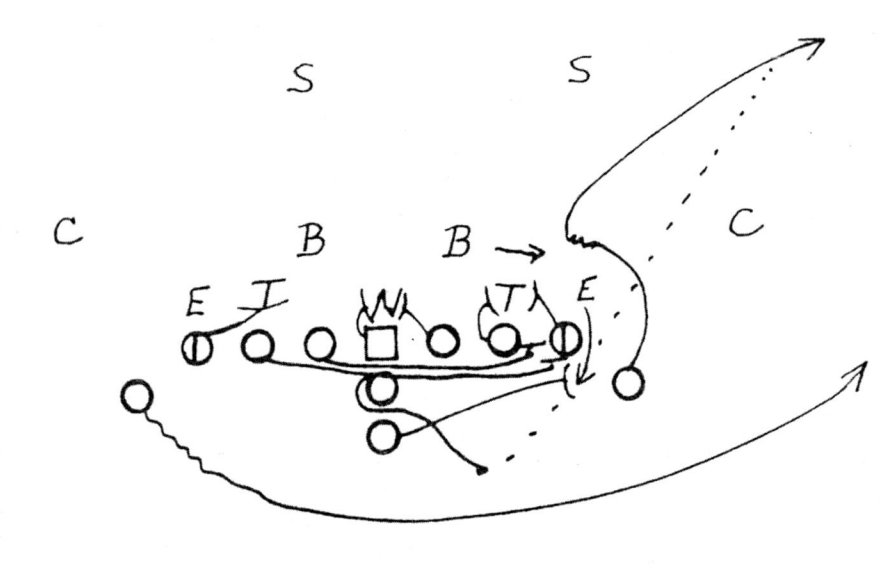

DIAGRAM 12-1   14 TOSS PASS VS. 5-2
Note: BLOCKED LIKE TOSS

Scissors Deep

The Scissors Pass series, mentioned earlier in Chapter 8, is designed to give you a *wheel* effect, with patterns in layers short to deep (Diagram 12-2). However, if you begin to see loaded fronts dedicated to stopping the run and leaving only one or two safeties deep, you can call "18 Scissors Deep" (Diagram 12-3), which tells all receivers to run 9's ("go" patterns). The quarterback can then have his choice of open receivers and score "six" very quickly.

Another way to enhance the scissors series and add a little fun is to actually hand it off to the wing who fakes a sweep for several steps, then stops, rotates, and throws it back to the quarterback doing a swing pattern (Diagram 12-4). This is a super goal-line play.

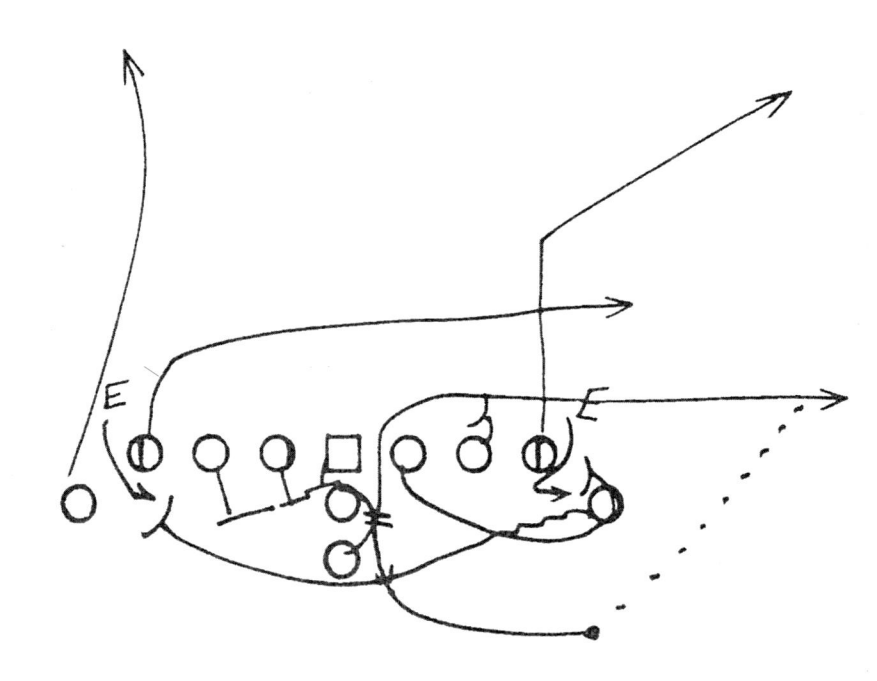

DIAGRAM 12-2   18 SCISSORS PASS

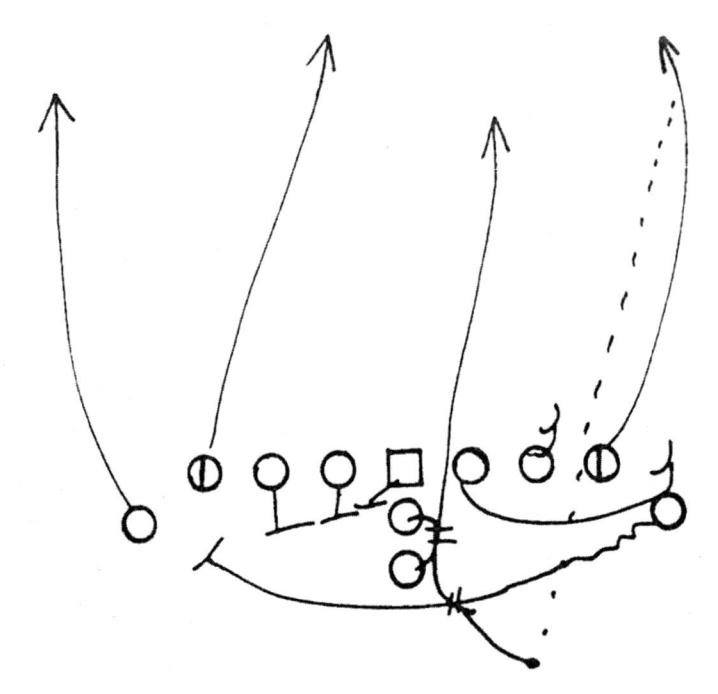

Diagram 12-3 18 Scissors Pass "Deep"

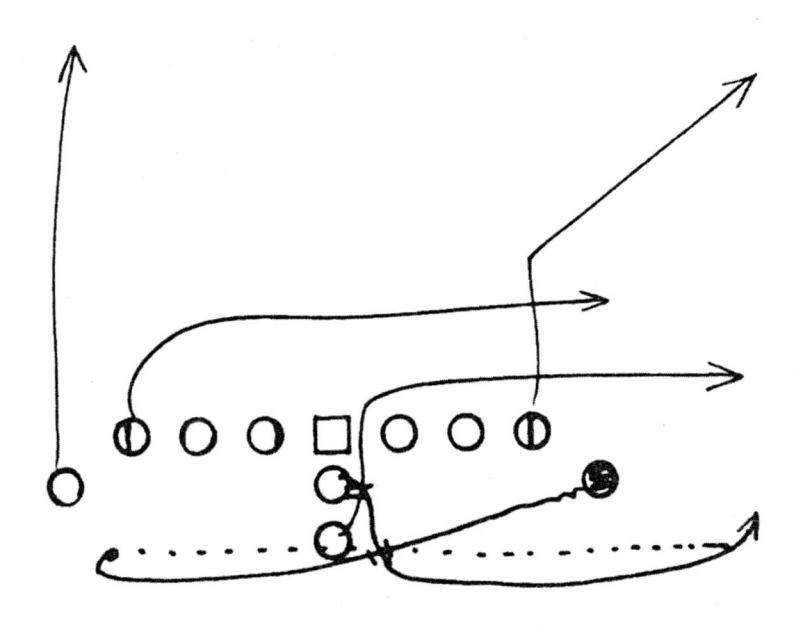

Diagram 12-4 18 Scissors Pass—"QB Throwback"

Advanced Double Wing Passing Plays

Speed Pass

The next play is a combination of the No-Play Pass where the wing motions out to the sideline before running a streak and 24 (Toss) pass action. The blocking is aggressive throughout. The backside tight end stays home. The onside tight end runs an immediate sideline (arrow) route. The onside wing runs a post. The fullback seals the playside defensive end. The motion wing changes speeds on this play. He must sprint (the same way he would do in the "fly" motion) to the sideline. This should catch the defense off guard, especially if they have crowded their corners inside. The defense has been lulled into seeing the normal wing motion play after play, and now it sees this guy flying outside! The corner will be chasing hard to catch up. The quarterback reverses out and rolls behind the fullback's block. He should be looking at the streaking wing first, the post wing second, and, if needed, the tight end's arrow third. This is called "24 Speed Pass" for obvious reasons.

A couple of coaching notes: Try to run this to the field (wide) side and if you desire, change the count to 4 or 5 to decoy a no-play (Diagram 12-5).

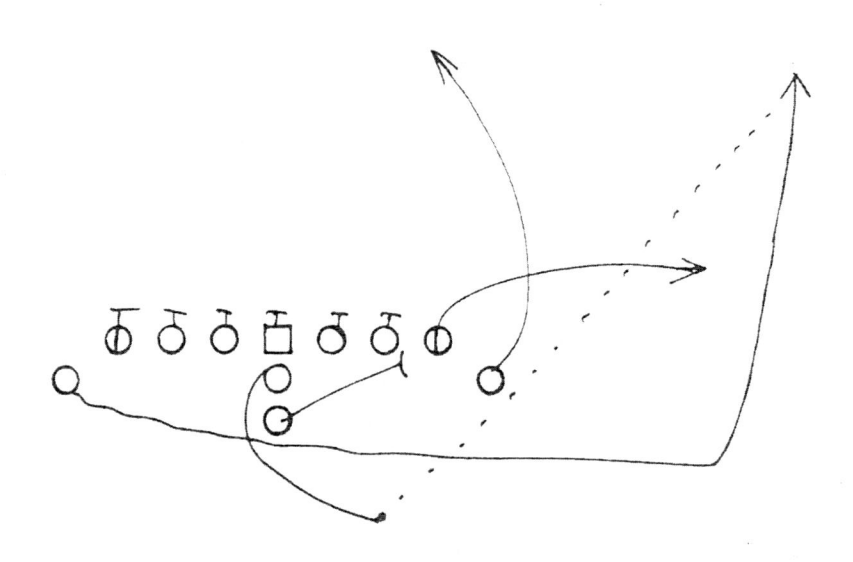

Diagram 12-5   24 Speed Pass

Reverse Pass

The last play is a wild one. It's our version of the old Double Reverse Pass. On a 24 reverse pass the line will block aggressively. The fullback blocks the onside defensive end. The offside tight end runs a post pattern. The quarterback, after giving the ball to the 4-back, runs an out in the flat. The 4-back gives the ball to the 2-back who fakes the run for a few steps and then sets up behind the fullback's block. He should look for the tight end as primary, the quarterback's out as secondary, or he can take off and run as the third option (Diagram 12-6).

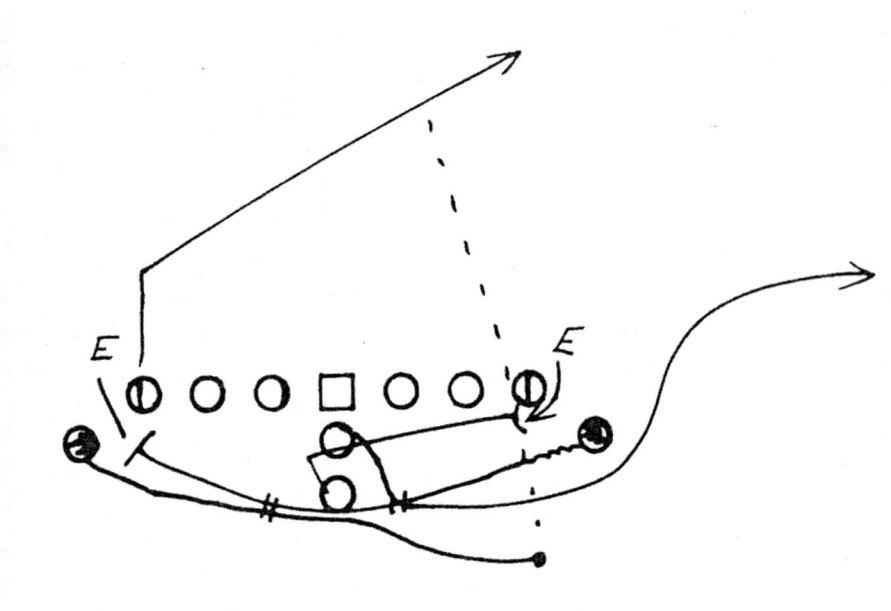

DIAGRAM 12-6 24 REVERSE PASS

A Final Note on Personnel

If your wings happen to be your better receivers, you can flip-flop the pattern sets with the tight ends. This tactic allows the tight ends to run the clearing routes as decoys and your wings to get the ball on the drags, curls, and corner routes.

Chapter 13

I-Formation: Change Can be Good

The more things change, the more they remain the same.
—Alphonse Karr

Earlier on, I emphasized the need to keep things simple. The double wing helps you keep the same formation, the same type of motion, and snap count. Even the beginning of each play has a similar look. This sameness allows you to reduce mistakes to almost zero. It also allows you to simplify everything. The deception factor, however, is still very much a part of your offensive scheme. The defense cannot identify any play by tendencies: They begin to overreact to "The Toss," ("The hub of the wheel") and the cross toss, sweep, and cut become extremely effective. So why change the formation?

It has been our experience that the defense gets into sort of a groove. Even if they don't change their set, they become double wing conscious. If they are supplied with excellent personnel and have done a good job scouting you, they may begin to slow your offense's progress. It does not happen very often, but as I've said before, there are times when the defense just has your number. It is times like these that switching to the I-formation can really put you back in the driver's seat (Diagram 13-1).

Going to the I-formation is like going back to the future, so to speak. The toss action was birthed out of the "I." Many championships have been won and records broken by offenses running it. To recommend change seems contradictory after I have doggedly emphasized staying basic, but the beauty of the I-formation is that you run the exact same plays (for the most part), and use the same technique as that in the double wing.

We run mostly double tight end with a wide flanker (Diagram 13-1). The line is set the same. The quarterback and fullback are the same. The tailback is set about 10 yards deep (if slower maybe 7-8 yards). The flanker is set as wide as possible, depending on the play. We designate the flanker formation by calling, "I-Right (or Left), 24 Toss." The tailback becomes the 2-back and flanker is now the 4-back.

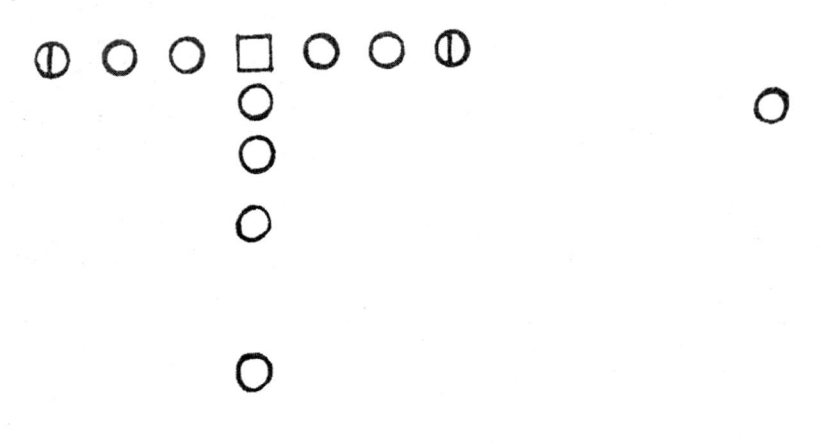

DIAGRAM 13-1 DOUBLE TE—"I" FORMATION

Advantages of the I-formation are several. The first being, as mentioned before, is that the defense must now deal with a whole new animal. If the defense has slowed the double wing, it is because they have somehow begun to guess right and adjust properly. The double wing, as a whole, is primarily a horizontal attack offense (at least on the onset of each play). If the defense has stopped it, they probably have great personnel, have filled each gap, and have enough speed to force most plays wide.

The I-formation is a definite vertical offense. It is this single factor that makes changing to it a good option. If you have a good tailback who is durable enough and aggressive enough to dish out punishment, you can blast the defense into submission again. By placing the tailback 10 yards deep, you give him a tremendous head start. By the time he hits the line, he will be at full speed!

RUNNING TO DAYLIGHT.

Another advantage is that the defense has to adjust to something new. Even though it is still a double tight end set, they must honor the flanker. It is amazing how much this change in formation causes the defense to loosen up. By doing this you get a nice reprieve from the overloaded fronts.

The defense, unlike the offense, must spend practice time working on different schemes for the double wing *and* the "I." Since the plays and techniques remain similar for the offense, it does not take away from *our* preparation time.

You may switch to the "I" for only a series and then jump back to the double wing, but it has been our experience that the defense gets out of sync just enough to start popping big gains again. It is strange, but it just messes up the consistency of even a dominant defense. The change catches the defense off balance and undermines their confidence.

The last advantage to this formation switch would be to feature personnel. These advantages will be addressed in the next couple of chapters.

Finally, there is an array of I-formation sets that you may want to use. Don Markham made the stack-I famous before he converted to the double wing (Diagram 13-2). We have used a twin set (Diagram 13-3) when we had good receivers. Another Markham gadget is the offset fullback set (Diagram 13-4) that we call seven formation. It utilizes a lot of fullback motion to gain an edge on the defense's flank. Some teams even employ an unbalanced trips look (Diagram 13-5) or a tight end spread set (Diagram 13-6). In choosing any of these, you must keep personnel and practice time in mind as a guide to how or why you want it as another option. Many of the same plays mentioned can be run out of all of these with a few adjustments.

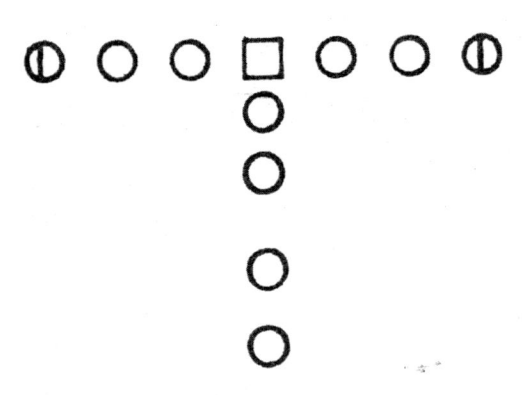

DIAGRAM 13-2   DOUBLE TE—STACK-I FORMATION

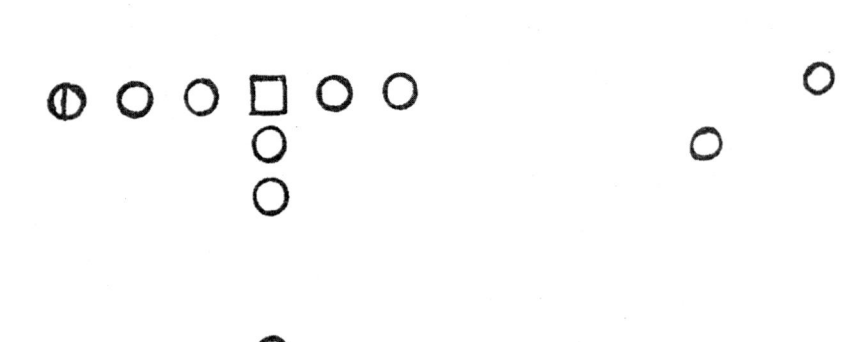

DIAGRAM 13-3   I-TWINS

I-Formation: Change Can be Good

Diagram 13-4 "7" Formation

Diagram 13-5 Unbalanced Trips

Diagram 13-6 Double TE Spread

Chapter 14

I-Formation Running Plays: Feature Back

It is fatal to enter any war without the will to win it.
—Douglas MacArthur

The best thing about the I-Formation is that it allows you to feature your best running back. University of Southern California, AKA "Tailback U," gained a place in college football history by featuring the best tailbacks in the country. It is downright fun to watch a tailback tear up a defense play after play. A good, tough back can run the ball 30-40 times a game. David Dotson carried 54 times (the California state single-game record) for Leo Brouhards' 1989 Moreno Valley team. Marshawn Thompson ran it 375 times in a single season (third best in the state) for Mark Pettingill's 1989 Bassett team. These are just a few examples of what the I-toss has produced in the past.

The California state record book is filled with names of players who were fortunate enough to be able to run in an offense using this concept. (For more on the records, see the Appendix.) Suffice it to say, it works and it works well.

I-Toss

The first play that can be run from the I-formation is the main play; that is, the I-toss. The blocking scheme is exactly like the double wing except for the flanker, who can block the corner, the safety, even the linebacker (utilizing motion if desired). You may want to set him away from the play side as a decoy. The advantage of the "I" set is that the tailback has room to accelerate toward the line and has a great view of where things are opening up. Our backs tell us it's like standing on a hill; you can see everything. Also by attacking in a vertical direction the back has greater potential to choose any lane, especially the cutback (Diagram 14-1).

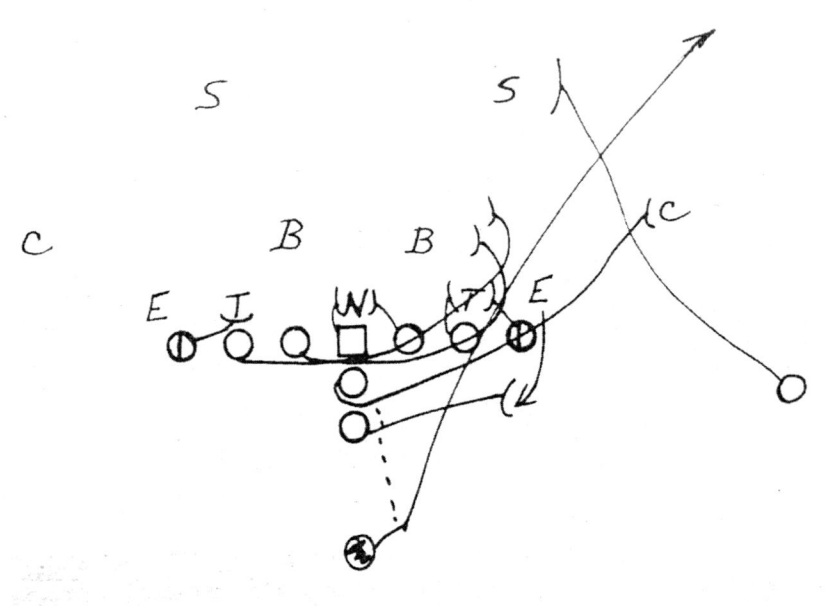

DIAGRAM 14-1 I-Toss vs. 5-2

I-Cut

As you begin to pound away at the defense, they will respond by crowding the line of scrimmage and by overreacting to flow, in an effort to pursue the ball. This is where you would run the I-cut (Diagram 14-2). Keep in mind that the fullback is still as close as he can possibly be to the quarterback. In a sense, he is hidden. The defense's focus is on the tailback. So again as in double wing we have the "disappearing man trick."

The difference is that now you want to show toss and not sweep. Everything will give the appearance of toss. The quarterback reverses out, gives an inside handoff to the fullback, then fakes toss action. The tailback fakes receiving the pitch

I-FORMATION RUNNING PLAYS: FEATURE BACK 107

and drives in the line, going for 10 full yards with his fake. The other difference is the flanker, who can either block the corner back or neutralize him off by running a pattern.

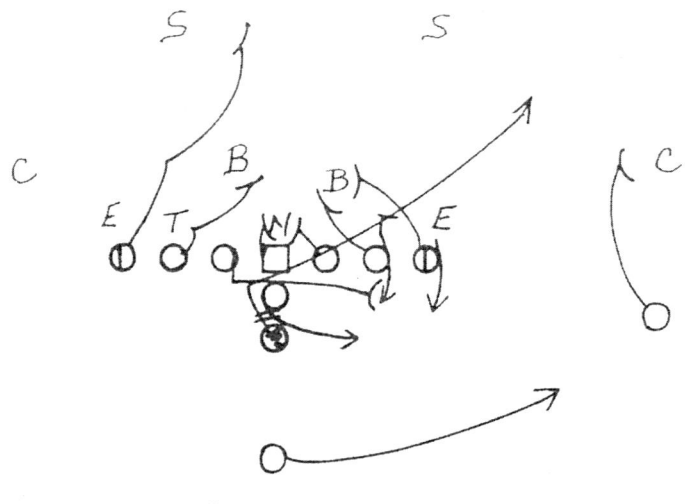

DIAGRAM 14-2 I-CUT VS. 5-2

NOTHING BETTER THAN OPEN FIELD.

I-Sweep

To go outside with the "I" can be difficult because of the lack of deception among other things. The tailback can be seen trying to run the sweep a mile away. So it is not by trickery, but by sheer force that you gain the outside flank. The sweep blocking can be altered to fit your personnel and/or the defensive scheme. The most effective way, we have seen, is to have the flanker crack back on the defensive end (with motion if desired). The onside tight end downs the defensive tackle. The onside tackle downs the linebacker. The center seals his nose. The back-side tackle and tight end go downfield. Both guards pull as wide as possible. The onside guard gets the corner back, and the back-side guard stops the next defensive threat. The fullback and quarterback also help lead up. The tailback must go far enough on his horizontal route to allow time for the blocking to set up (Diagram 14-3).

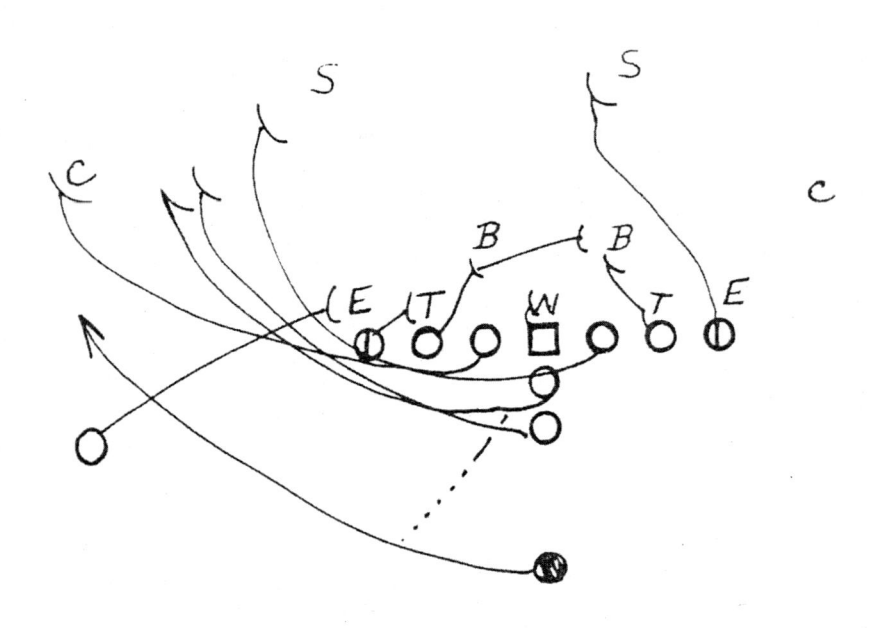

Diagram 14-3 I-Sweep vs. 5-2

I-Trap

The last play we use from this formation is something you can't do in a double wing. The I-trap is blocked just like cross toss or reverse, except for the flanker who can be either away from the play (Diagram 14-4) or to the play (Diagram 14-5) where he again either blocks the corner back or runs him off with a decoy pattern. The deception comes from the backfield action. The fullback takes a tight route past the quarterback, up and through the vacated back side. The tailback takes a jab step in the fullback's direction, then plants and cuts back with his inside elbow up. He should take the handoff and find his pulling escorts. He runs up inside the guard's kick-out block. This play has not been a world beater for us, but if for no other reason, it helps set up the trap pass which has been a game breaker.

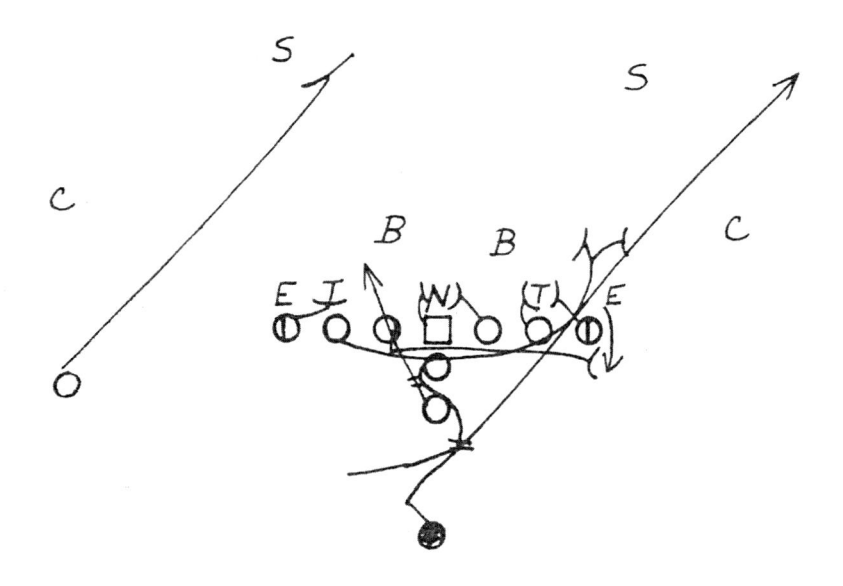

DIAGRAM 14-4 I-TRAP VS. 5-2

110 Chapter 14

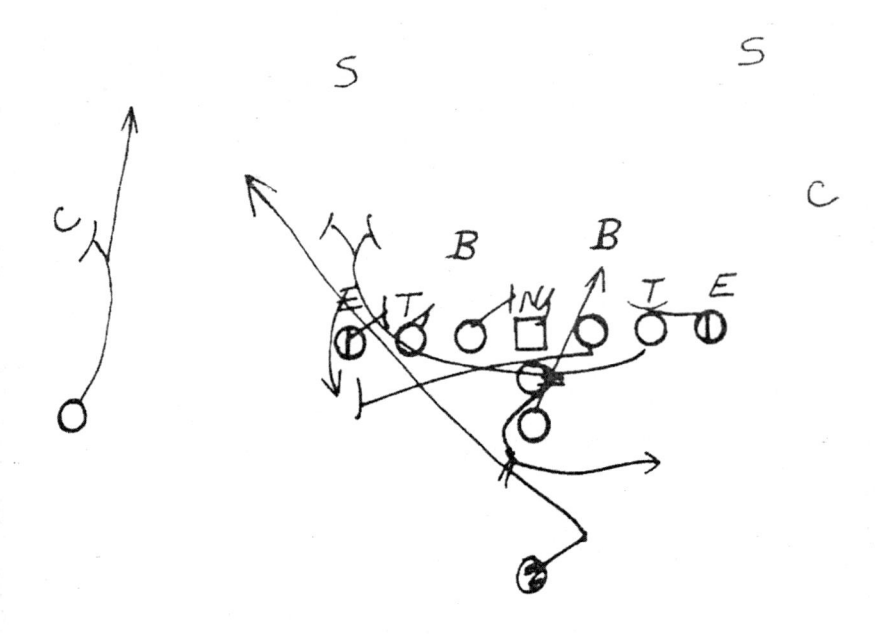

DIAGRAM 14-5   I-TRAP VS. 5-2

The toss, cut and sweep out of the "I" can be enough to win a season full of games. The blocking patterns, as you have seen, are the same or at least similar to the double wing. The main difference is the vertical explosion of the I-toss. But mainly it puts the game in the hands of your best back.

Chapter 15

I-Formation Passing Plays: Feature Receiver

If he has talent and cannot use it, he has failed.
—Thomas Wolfe

The motivation to run the I-formation may be to put the ball in the hands of your best players. Your best player may be the tailback or it could be a receiver. Since the double wing utilizes two tight ends, the true wide receiver type of player must either be converted to wing or play defense. However, with the "I" you can now find a home for your all-star receiver. We at Foothill are devoted to the double wing and have had the running backs who allowed us to do it well. But if we had a high school version of San Francisco 49ers' all-pro wide receiver Jerry Rice, we would use a formation with a place for him to excel. If you have several wide receiver types, you may want to consider the twin-I or spread or even some form of trips, and still run some semblance of the toss offense.

Even if you don't have a feature receiver, the passing game out of the I-formation can be fantastic, just throwing to any eligible receiver. The advantage you gain by keeping the two tight ends is that they allow you to keep the same overload concept when running the ball. The defense must remain concentrated in the box (tight end to tight end). They must also respect a good receiver. The I-formation forces the defense to prioritize what it will stop. This makes for easy reads by the quarterback.

Chapter 15

I-Trap Pass

Our favorite passing play is the trap pass. As mentioned, the actual trap has not been a big gainer, but by running it even once, it allows us to freeze the defense enough to throw the play action pass effectively. In "I-Left, 24 Trap Pass" (Diagram 15-1), the left tackle and guard pull to the right to decoy a trap. The center, right guard, and tackle all do an aggressive pivot block to decoy run and then to seal their men away from the quarterback. The fullback slips past the quarterback and runs a shallow out in the flat. The tailback fakes trap action to the right (after jab step). He should carry out his fake for 10 yards. The right tight end runs a drag. The left tight end runs a corner route, and the wide receiver (4-back) runs a post. The quarterback reverses out, rotating 180°, faking a toss. He then will roll away, taking *three* giant steps backward hiding the ball against his belly.

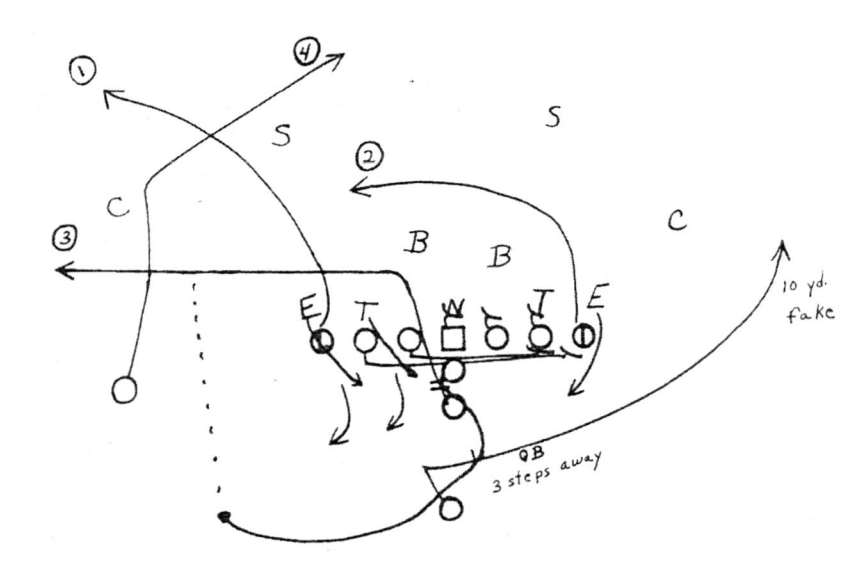

Diagram 15-1 I-Left, 24 Trap Pass vs. 5-2

Without the quarterback taking the three steps back, the defense will not buy the fake. You must emphasize it, or the quarterback will get killed. By going deep and away the quarterback will not only sell the trap fake, but will have enough distance to roll out beyond the defensive end and defensive tackle who are almost always in a shallow "B-line" pursuit. The 49ers have perfected this play into an art form. It is our most effective passing weapon. It may seem risky to pull the whole back side away and release four men on patterns, but we have not been sacked yet. The defense always sucks up and our quarterback has plenty of room and time as he begins to roll out. He should look at the corner *first*, then the drag, and then the flat. He can, if given instructions in the huddle, go to the post, but it is a tough throw. The other obvious choice is to take off and run.

I-Scissors

The other combination pass play is similar to our scissors pass in double wing. The difference is that the fullback will now stay and fill for the pulling onside guard, and the tailback will block the back-side defensive end. The offside tight end stills runs a drag, the onside flanker runs a streak, and the onside tight end runs an out. The quarterback fakes to the fullback and tailback, then rolls behind the guard's block. He should look deep to short (Diagram 15-2).

I-Pitch Pass

The sucker play category would not be complete without the toss (pitch) pass. Just like the other running back passing plays, we set it up by pounding the I-Toss, then have the tail back pull up and throw. The "24 Pitch Pass" is run exactly like "24 Toss" but the offensive line knows not to go down field. The quarterback will turn and protect back-side, and the fullback will get onside. The 4-back will fake a stalk block on the safety, then turn and run for the corner. The tailback will sell the run, stop, hit the corner route or throw it out of bounds. If the receiver is covered and he has pressure, he can also run for daylight (Diagram 15-3).

114 Chapter 15

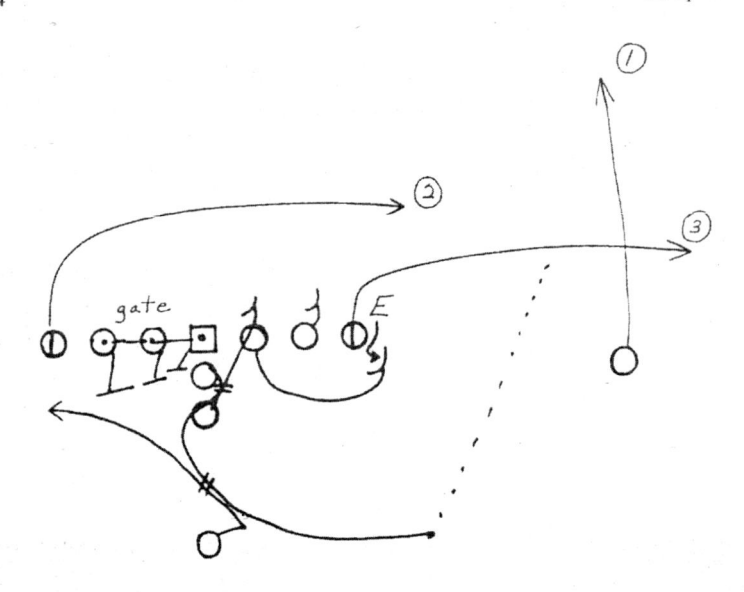

Diagram 15-2 I-Right 18 Scissors Pass

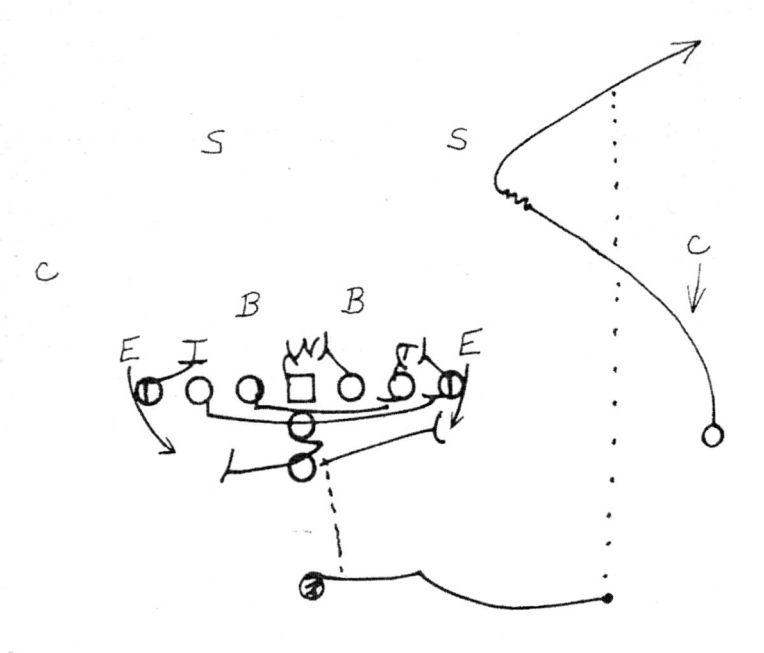

Diagram 15-3 I-Right Pitch Pass

Finally, we have our isolation series that puts the ball into your best receiver's hands. We call this our gold series. Gold to our lineman means quick release or P.P. blocking. We will usually put our flanker to the wide side to allow for more freedom. We will gain ample respect for our running attack by pounding the defense with it for the majority of the game. Also, in keeping with our philosophy, we will not throw on obvious passing downs. We will sprinkle the pass in with our overall attack. This will make the defense prioritize—mainly to put most of their men into the box. Even if they know we have a great receiver, it will be hard to justify giving up two defensive backs when we are gaining 5-8 yards a crack on the ground. This means you have a great athlete (you hope) single covered to the wide side.

ALL ALONE BEHIND THE DEFENSE.

Fade

The fade is the most obvious way to gain big yards fast (Diagram 15-4). The fullback always blocks left and the tailback always blocks right. The line (tight end to tight end) P.P. blocks, and the quarterback takes a one-step drop and releases the ball to a designated spot. The release must be as high as possible and the ball must be placed where the receiver can either get it, or be in good position to protect it from being intercepted.

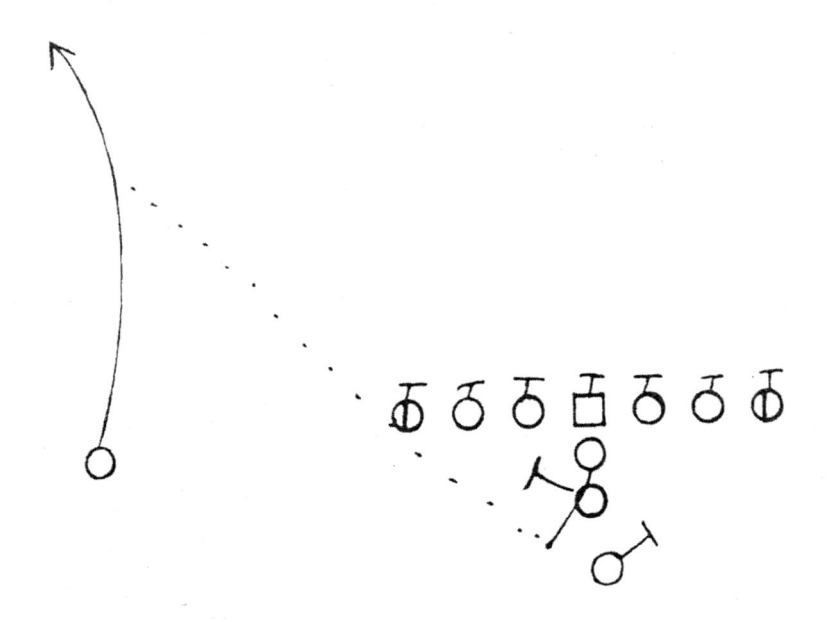

DIAGRAM 15-4 I-LEFT GOLD FADE

Comeback

Off of the fade, we can run a comeback route (Diagram 15-5) once we have the corner back playing off enough. The receiver should drive hard to the corner back's outside shoulder, then stop and angle back toward the sideline. (Remember to line up, leaving enough room to the outside).

Slant

If the safety is playing extremely shallow or deep, the next pattern that you could employ would be the slant. The receiver must drive hard for the hole in the zone, turn his head inside quickly, and have his hands ready to catch the ball (Diagram 15-6).

I-FORMATION PASSING PLAYS: FEATURE RECEIVER

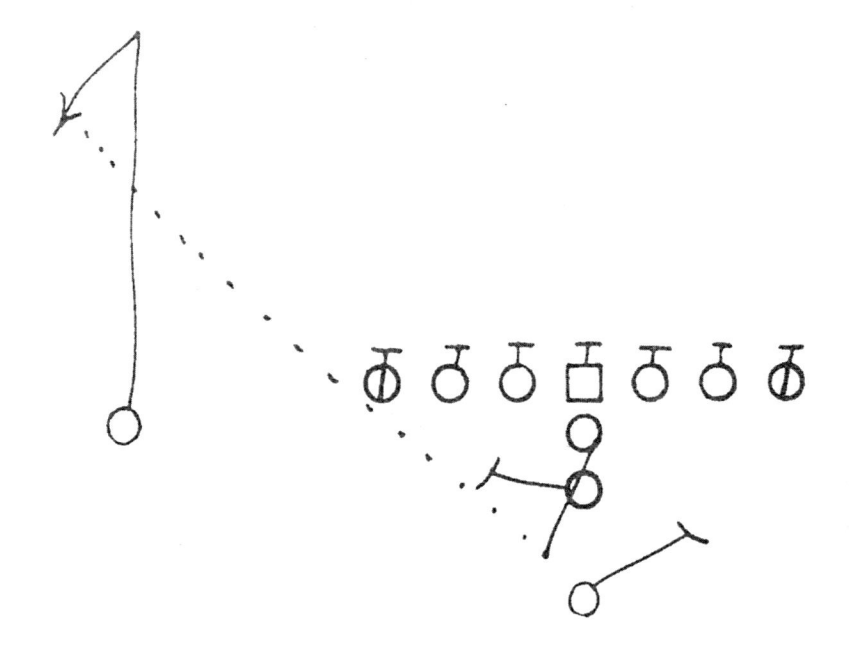

DIAGRAM 15-5 I-LEFT GOLD COMEBACK

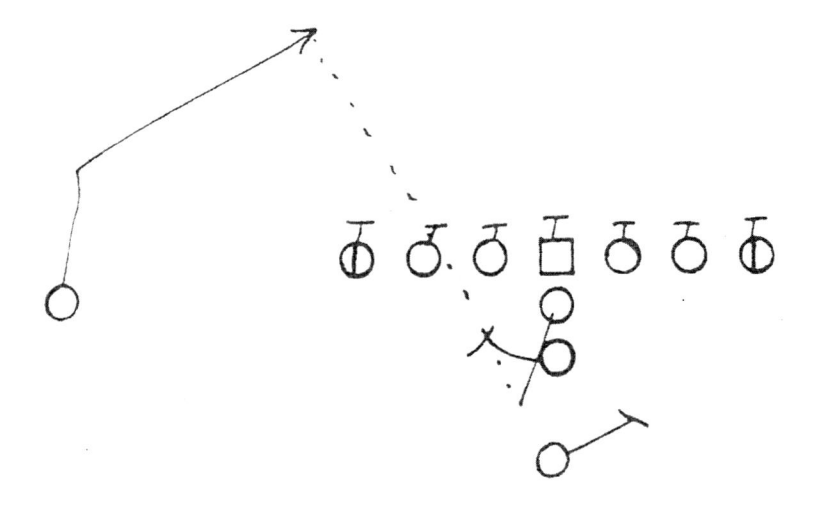

DIAGRAM 15-6 I-LEFT GOLD SLANT

Hitch

The last pattern we use is the hitch (Diagram 15-7). In order to even consider this one, you must have a pretty good (fast) athlete at receiver, and the corner must be playing soft. The receiver will take a false drive step, then stop and rotate his body toward the quarterback with his hands ready. The quarterback should zip the ball low and hard. Should he fail, it could easily give the defense an interception leading to a quick six points. This play can be run to the short side with good results. The onside of the line (tight end to guard) will P.P. block, then quickly get up and charge out in front of the receiver, who will try to cut underneath this wall of blockers.

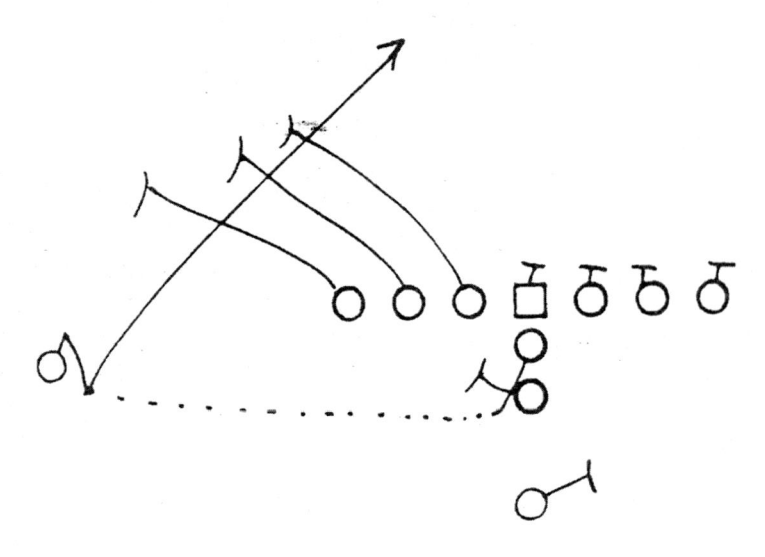

Diagram 15-7 I-Left Gold Hitch

Our passing game is not based on innovative genius. We do not ask our athletes to make a lot of adjustments other than basic reads by the quarterback and the receiver. However, the very fact that we are not dependent on the pass makes it more effective. Analogous to a boxer's flurry in the middle of a match, we can throw a barrage of right hands (running game), which will create an opening for a devastating left hook (passing game).

Chapter 16

STACK-I FORMATIONS: BRING DOWN THE HAMMER

When you are an anvil, hold still;
when you are a hammer, strike your fill.
—George Herbert

The stack-I formation is different from both the double wing and the regular I-formation, yet it contains the same elements that make the other two so successful. The basic plays can be run: toss, sweep, and the cut. The cross toss or reverse cannot be run for obvious reasons, but you can run a trap and a tight end reverse to assist your counter attack. The formation (Diagram 16-1) is the same tight end to tight end. The quarterback and fullback don't change either. The 4-back or "stackback" bears resemblance to a tightened up I-back, approximately 2-3 yards back from the 3-back (fullback). The tail back is anywhere from 8-10 yards deep depending on the play and his speed.

Out of all the formations we feel this is the "muscle" set. If you can get some fairly large athletes at the fullback and stackback positions, then you can really bludgeon defenses on a consistent basis because of the dynamics of this formation. "The Toss" concepts remain; you put more blockers at the point of attack. The concept is further enhanced by the vertical thrust of the I-style offense. It is also surprisingly efficient at getting outside on defenses. It is simple enough and close enough in philosophy to the other sets to make it worth having as a back-up attack. Looking back at the history of this offense shows that the stack-I was actually a mainstay of the originators of "The Toss" attack.

① 〇 〇 □ 〇 〇 ①
   ¹ 〇 QB
   ³ 〇 FB
   ⁴ 〇 Stack

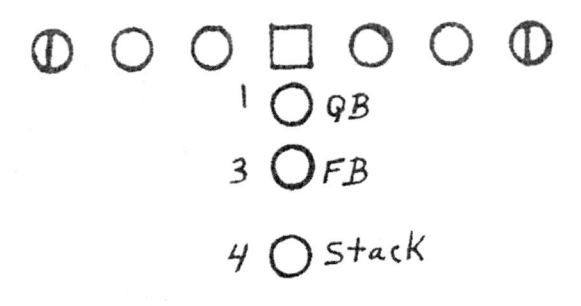

   ² 〇 Tail

DIAGRAM 16-1   STACK-I FORMATION

Stack-Toss

The first play (as always) is the toss. The toss is the same as the regular I-toss, but you get an extra blocker inside (Diagram 16-2.) An important coaching point: The stackback needs to take the same crossover step as the fullback in order to be out of the way of the pitch. At first you may find your quarterback bouncing the ball off the 4-back's helmet, but keep pushing the crossover, and you will get it right.

The stackback will attack the safety, or whoever shows up as an immediate threat. Everyone else does the same as in the regular I formation. The tailback needs to work his approach to the hole. He may need to get deeper, because if he's quick and impatient, he may get to the point of attack before the mass of blockers have effectively cleared the way. The play takes a few more seconds to break open because of all the bodies involved.

Stack-Switch

An alternative technique is to run a "switch." The fullback and stackback can trade assignments to keep the defensive end guessing. The "stackback" can catch the defensive end by surprise, and the fullback has no problem getting quickly to the safety (Diagram 16-3).

STACK-I FORMATIONS: BRING DOWN THE HAMMER 121

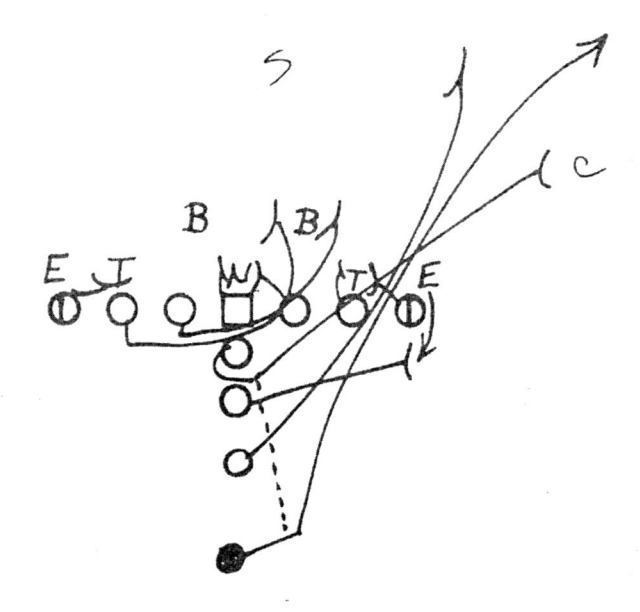

DIAGRAM 16-2   24 TOSS VS. 5-2

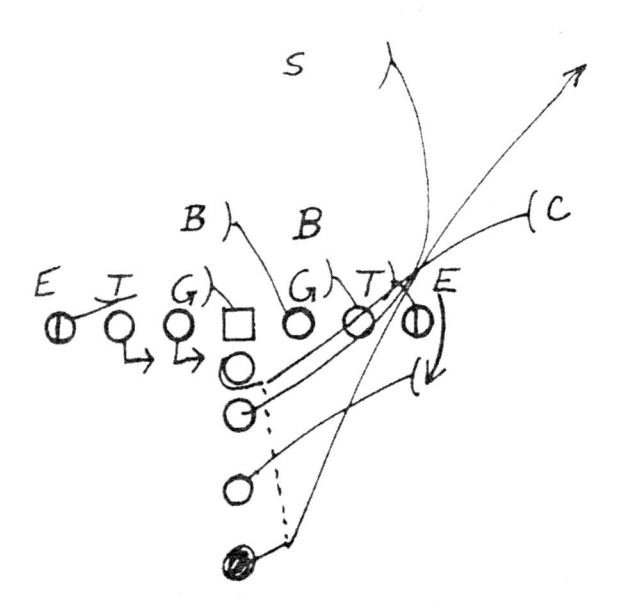

DIAGRAM 16-3   24 TOSS "SWITCH" VS. 6-2

Stack-Sweep

We like the toss, but out of the stack, we love the sweep. Our main uniform color is red, so we affectionately call this play "red river right" or "red river left." Technically it is 28 and 29 Sweep, but one of our opponent's coaches called it "black and blue" left and right. It is really something to see on film: it looks very much like a kickoff return wedge! (Diagram 16-4).

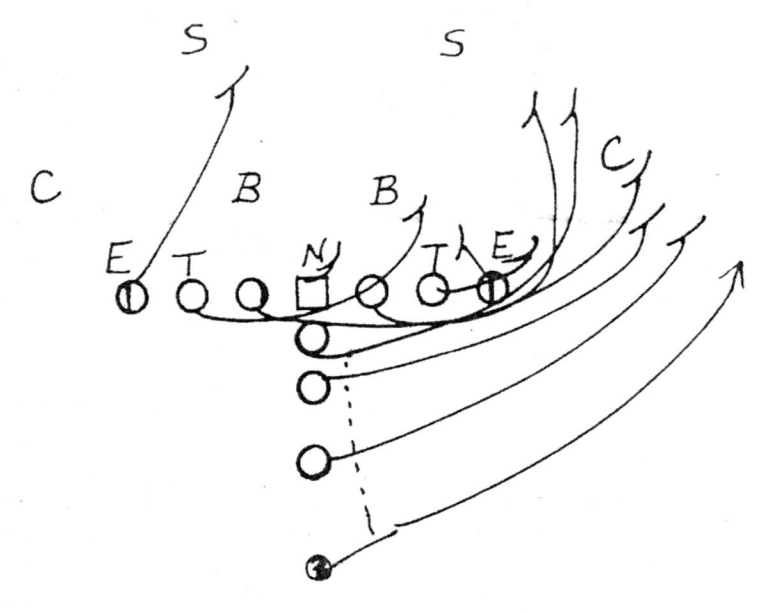

Diagram 16-4   28 Sweep ("Red River Right") vs. 5-2

We pull four linemen and lead with three backs. If your math skills are decent, it means that you add a total of seven guys at the point of attack. The play begins at the onside tight end who down blocks the defensive tackle. The onside tackle's block is very tricky; he must take a step toward the defensive end with his outside foot at a 45% angle. Then he must go to an immediate bear crawl and aim his head at the far thigh pad of the defensive end. He must continue to crawl and attempt to cut his man or hook his body around in front, keeping the defensive end pinned in so he cannot contain or pursue the sweep. The onside guard pulls way wide to trap the corner back inside. The center pivot blocks the nose. The offside guard pulls around the corner and takes the first threat. The off tackle pulls and cleans up any leaks created by the onside vacating.

The back-side tight end goes downfield to block a safety, while the quarterback rotates, pitches to the tailback, and leads around the corner. The fullback and stackback cross over and lead around the corner. All these blockers must be taught to run right at the buckle of the defender and take him wherever he wants to go. It is imperative to discourage them from reaching (outside the shoulders) or grabbing cloth and also to avoid clipping. The angle in which they take on defenders will vary. They should attempt to shove their guy to the inside and give the runner a path down the sideline, but this is the ideal situation. There are many times (especially when the play is run toward the bench) where the tail back runs out of grass and must cut up field; so like a kickoff return, all the blockers need to do is maintain contact and let the back pick his lane.

Stack-Cut

The cut is obviously set up by the success of the sweep. The defense that is flying to stop the sweep won't be home for a trap. The concept remains the same as always. The tailback and stackback both fly outside to sell the sweep. The fullback does the same step and follows the guard through the back door (Diagram 16-5).

Stack-Lead

The lead is unique to this formation. It becomes a kind of counter play when used after running the sweep often enough to make the defense become perimeter conscious. We like to cross block at the point of attack regardless of whether the defense is using an odd or even front, to get better blocking angles. We isolate the linebacker with the fullback's block. Everybody else just man blocks (Diagram 16-6). After several successful sweeps (or even tosses), we get the defense in a pursuit mode and the lead blocker splits a defense that is not set up to plug the middle.

124　　　　　　　　　　　　　　　　　　　　　　　　　　Chapter 16

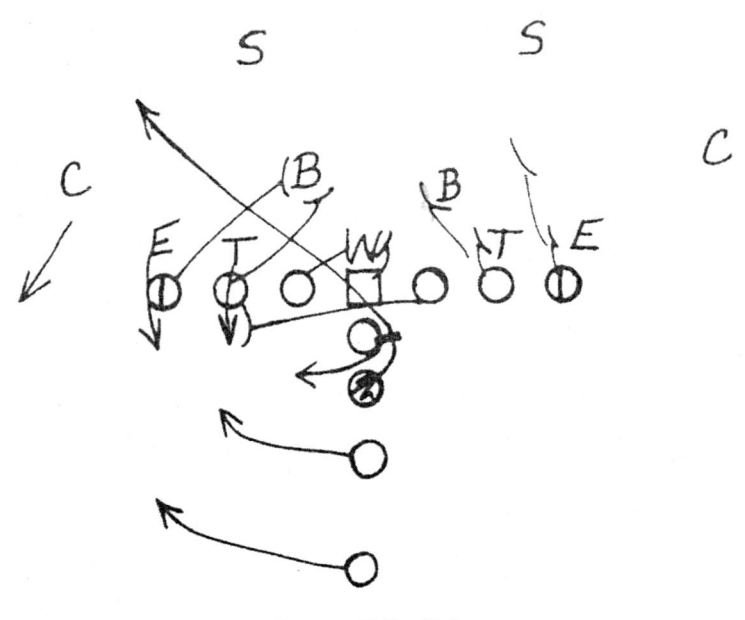

Diagram 16-5　31 Cut

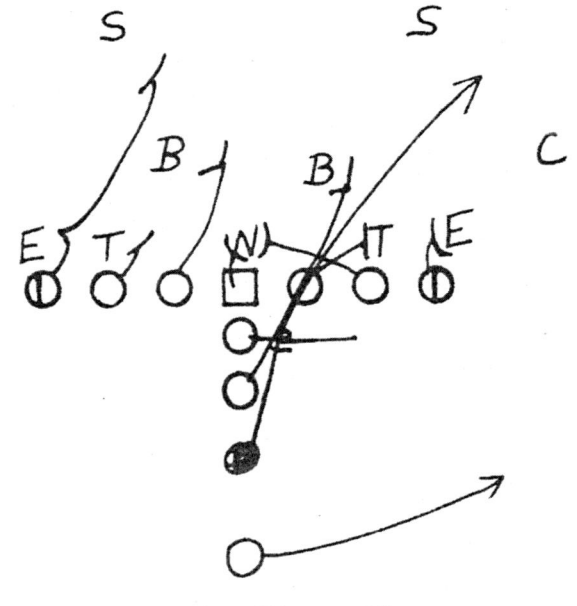

Diagram 16-6　42 Lead vs. 5-2

Stack-Trap

The stack brings a whole lot of man power to an isolated area. It is extremely dynamic and nothing is better at exploiting a defensive physical weakness. It is very direct, but it is not without its counters. The trap is the one used the most. The trap from a stack formation is blocked like the cross toss but is enhanced by both the fullback and the stackback going away from the point of attack. If the sweep and toss are effective, then you will really catch pursuit flow crosswise. If the block on the defensive end is decent, then the tailback can spring for big yards (Diagram 16-7).

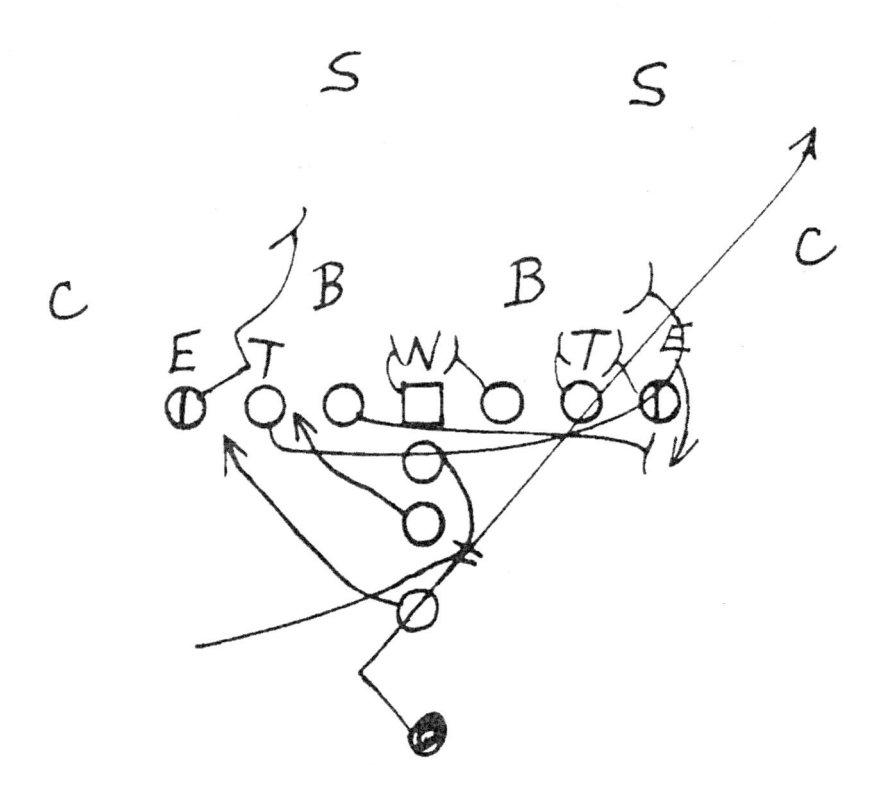

DIAGRAM 16-7   24 TRAP VS. 5-2

126 Chapter 16

Stack-Tight End Reverse

The other counter to the stack gets the ball to your tight end without requiring a pass. The tight end reverse has the onside part of the offensive line down blocking, the center filling, and the off guard doing the kickout on the defensive end. The three backs show sweep action on the opposite side of the play. The quarterback reverses out, pivots, making a 360% turn, and gives the ball underneath to the left tight end (Diagram 16-8). The line of scrimmage gets so congested that the tight end cannot be seen until he pops out on the other side. If your tight ends are good runners, then this is an excellent way to use them. The stack-I doesn't lend itself to running back counters for obvious reasons, so the tight end reverse serves as this purpose.

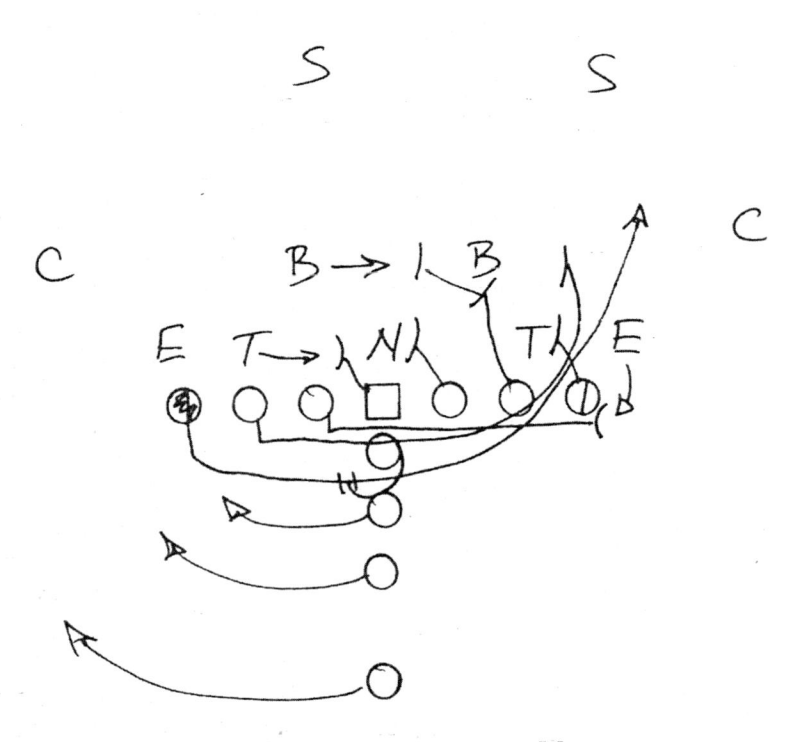

DIAGRAM 16-8 68 TE REVERSE VS. 5-2

THE STACK-I CAUSES ANOTHER TRAIN WRECK.

Stack-Trap Pass

The only pass play we throw out of the stack is the trap pass. We false key by pulling the tackle and guard away from the quarterback's roll. This gets the defensive line chasing the tackle and guard and allows our quarterback to roll in the clear. The center, off guard, and off tackle pass block aggressively, pivoting their men to the outside gap. The onside tight end runs a corner route. The offside tight end runs a deep drag. The fullback slips into the flat, while the stackback fakes a lead block and pins the defensive end in to ensure that the quarterback has enough time to throw.

The tailback jab steps toward the two lead blocks, then cuts back and carries out a handoff fake. The tailback can (after faking past the line of scrimmage) go down the sideline on a go pattern, if we feel it's open. The quarterback reverses out, fakes to the tailback—takes three big steps away from the line of scrimmage—then continues to roll deep and to the outside looking from deep to short (corner, drag, flat), or he can run if he is pressured (Diagram 16-9).

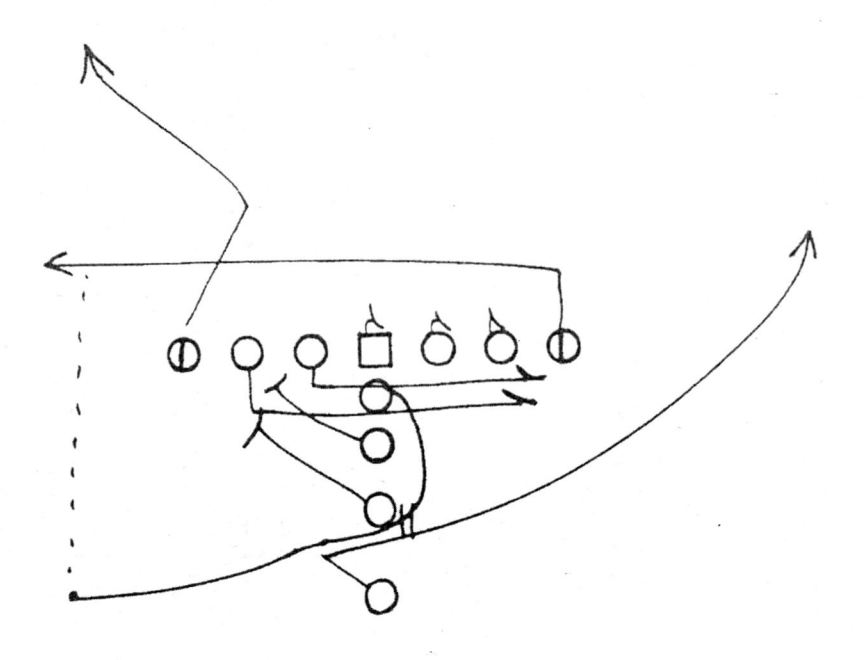

DIAGRAM 16-9   TRAP PASS

The counters and the trap pass are great change-ups, but the stack-I is not about being tricky. It is one of the few formations where your intentions are obvious and the defense has a pretty good idea of where you're going, but it just doesn't matter! Because the formation is balanced, the defense cannot get a strength call; and when the play begins, it is too late for the defense to stop the play because they are out-manned and overpowered at the point of attack. They cannot stack enough guys on the outside to stop the sweep. They cannot set enough men to stop the off-tackle toss, and if they get overaggressive in pursuit, then the cut, lead, trap, or tight end reverse ruins them! It stays within "The Toss" philosophy and is simple enough to use as an alternative attack without too much disruption to your practice schedule. On top of all this, it's a heck of a lot of fun to watch and run!

Part Five

The Players

The Ideal, Training & Motivation

Chapter 17

PERSONNEL: THE MOVING PARTS

> *Wars may be fought with weapons,*
> *but they are won by men.*
> —George S. Patton

When choosing athletes to fill certain positions, coaching preferences may vary. Of course, everybody loves the "regulars": size, speed, strength, ability, intelligence, desire, and coachable attitude. However, in choosing from these, especially on the high school level, a coach learns quickly that quite often you cannot have it all.

Coaches begin to make allowances in their minds for things they can live without. They also begin to look for qualities they feel are non-negotiable. I believe that certain qualities tie in to certain offenses. This may seem obvious to most, but you often see coaches who run offensive schemes that require certain personnel who they just do not have.

For instance, to run a traditional I-back offense, you must have dominating offensive linemen. Big, strong blockers are non-negotiable. You also have to have a tailback on whom you can depend to take a pounding and who also has break-away speed because he is your offense.

Special Qualities Are not Needed

The reason I mention this is because "The Toss" is unusual when it comes to needing a lot of special qualities. It is less personnel-dependent than any other offense I have ever encountered. The wishbone is similar in a way. The reason the service academies have run the "bone" is because they often must play with smaller personnel. They also do not get as much time to practice the long, complicated schemes that other teams might be able to run. The problem with the wishbone is that you absolutely must have a great quarterback and at least decent speed at the running back position. These can be tough to find year after year at the high school level. This makes even the "bone" a personnel *dependent* offense.

Building the Perfect "Toss" Team

What I'm saying is that you can get by with having smaller, slower, and weaker players more often in "The Toss" scheme. I will, however, go ahead and describe what we would like as an ideal at each position. As a general rule, what we want in every player, in order of importance is attitude, speed, strength, and then size.

1. *Attitude is number one.* Every coach wants athletes who are there to learn and want to win. We want them to be coachable, touch, aggressive, and smart.

2. *Speed is second because it has won many games for us.* Speed on defense is an absolute must. Speed on offense turns first downs into touchdowns. I will take speed over size and strength anytime.

3. *Strength comes in third, but we do put a big emphasis on weightlifting.* We lift year round. We want our guys to get stronger and to develop explosiveness through lifting. We want to wear down our opponent.

4. *Size is the final consideration.* Size also is a product of the weight room. It is the last in line of priorities because we can win without it. We would give up size to gain speed, but put both together and you win big!!

You will notice that most of these qualities can be enhanced by a good off-season program, which is something else that we stress with our athletes.

Position-By-Position

Here is a line up of the ideal combination of attributes for each player if you're using "The Toss" scheme, beginning with the tight ends and going through all the positions to the quarterback:

Tight Ends

The tight ends in our scheme must be great blockers—period! In a double tight end set, there is no room for guys who will not stick their noses in and punish the defense. Our tight ends must also be able to catch, especially tough underneath routes where they will take some pounding. As for size, anywhere between 5'11" and 6'4", and 175 to 220 pounds is ideal.

Tackles

At the tackles we want guys who can really move. Since we pull the back-side quite often, these guys cannot be ponderous. They need to have quick feet and more than 40-yard-dash speed. We time our guys in a toss simulation drill using cones. We can easily see their ability to get off the line of scrimmage, change directions, and control their momentum. We do not ask our tackles to move people by themselves head up, so we can give up size. We have played with tackles as light as 170 pounds. The ideal would be about 5'10" to 6'3", and 180 to 250 pounds, as long as they can move.

Guards

Guards are our real weapons. They are the "killer elite" on almost every play. These guys must really enjoy contact. We time these players using the same cone drill that we use for tackles. Ideal size would be between 5'9" and 6'3", and 160 to 220 pounds. Now we have played athletes as light as 150 pounds, but they were very tenacious and had great body position skills.

Center

The center can afford to be slower. He can be, if necessary, heavy set. If we have a short, "squatty bodied" player, we try to find him a home at center where movement is not that essential. He must, however, be a good drive blocker because he must set the double-teams and fill block laterally. Ideal size can be anywhere from 5'6" to 6'0", and 185 to 300 pounds.

Wings

The wings are special. Your offensive style will depend on their talents. So, the more versatile they are, the better off your team will be. We have had small wings (5'6" and 135 pounds), and big ones (6'0" and 210 pounds). We have had to use slower athletes (5.4-second 40-yard dash), and we have been blessed with fast ones (4.5-second 40-yard dash.) We have had players who could not run a sweep because of their lack of speed but could really pound off tackle. We have also had some who were young (sophomores) or inexperienced and couldn't quite make it happen between tackles, but they could fly. Consequently, we shaped our offense around that skill. We are not afraid to rotate kids in for special situations. Ideally, you would like your wings to be able to do it all. It would be great if they could run inside and out, make vicious blocks, and also catch the ball; but chances are you'll get just a few of these players every ten years. So it is obvious that you need to utilize and capitalize on what the player can do well.

Fullbacks

Fullbacks need to be quick. They do not have to be blazers, although it would be nice. They need to be large enough and tough enough to kick out defensive ends. They should be tenacious enough to run up the middle for the tough yards. Ideal size would be about 6'0" and 200 pounds.

Quarterback

The quarterback does not have to be the super athlete that most offenses require. The more talented he is as a thrower and/or runner, the better your attack; but you can put a lesser athlete here as long as he has decent feet and good ball-handling skills. When you throw all play action passes, the need for a rocket-armed "frozen rope" throwing quarterback isn't vital.

THE IMPORTANT INGREDIENT.

As long as he can at least get the ball close to an open receiver, that's great! As Lou Holtz once said, "If the ball was a hand grenade, get it close enough to hurt someone."

If the kid can run, then you can write that into your offense, but it's optional. It would be nice for him to be able to block at least marginally in order to enhance the toss play.

What they really need is mechanics. Foot placement, pivots, roll out angles—these are essentials. These can be taught to most would-be quarterbacks. The magic really happens in his ability to handle fake handoffs, pitches, and throwing actions. This is non-negotiable.

Without good feet and ball control skills, your offense will never "leave the ground." The better the quarterback is at each little intricacy, the better each play runs.

Finally, the quarterback must be a leader. Not necessarily a yeller and screamer, but a respected leader. The team must believe it can go places with this guy at the helm. The coach must feel he can count on the quarterback for good decisions in tough times.

Overall, the team's members must mesh together. In this "team offensive" concept, it is essential to work eleven members into a single unit. This may sound like a cliché, but more than in any other offense, every individual counts on every play.

I will address practice schedules in Chapter 19, but a coaching point I'll mention here is that team offensive time will take up the majority of your practice time. Individual drill time is okay early on, but when the season opens, most of our time is spent practicing as a unit, whether it be versus air, blocking bags, or live competition.

Chapter 18

Making What You Have Better

There are two ways to build a team. Either you get better players, or you get the players you've got better.
—Bum Phillips

"If only we could recruit." This has probably slipped out of every high school coach's mouth at least once or twice. It can be frustrating looking at your lower-level teams and seeing very little that can help you in the near future. But since we cannot recruit better players, we must make the ones we have become the best they can possibly be.

I really believe you can create athletes (or at least make non-athletes functional as team players). We believe we get the most out of our players because of a consistent four-year training plan. I will break this plan into three major categories: training, special competitions, and motivation.

Training

I have touched on some of what we do concerning weightlifting and practice time in previous chapters, but this section will outline our overall pre-season training.

Weightlifting is, for us, the most important aspect of our whole program. We take roll call every workout, and we expect every football player to be there year round unless he's playing another sport. There are many different programs and workouts, but the key is consistency. Our workout program is simple and involves lifting exercises that simulate football actions:

bench press, power cleans, squats, and dead-lifts. We lift three days a week after school. Our players all come after school for nearly two hours on Mondays, Wednesdays, and Fridays. We also work on our explosion ability by engaging in plyometric exercises such as box jumping, dot drills, and vertical leaping. We try to get our athletes as much equipment as we can to help them improve their skills—not just heavy-duty weight training equipment, but "gadgets" as well. The point is to motivate them to work hard. We "speed-train" with parachutes, harnesses, and anything else we can get our hands on.

Besides all this, we usually play pick-up basketball two to three times a week. This may seem trivial, but we feel we can promote competitiveness and aggressiveness through these games.

Our winter and spring training culminates with two weeks of spring football drills. We use spring training to test our athletes in many areas. This will give us a true picture of what we have accomplished in the winter and spring and where we stand going into summer.

Competition

"Competition breeds excellence." We really believe in this statement, so much so, that we promote competition continually. It can be very dreary to train for more than eight months without ever competing. Next season might as well be ten years away (especially to a 16- or 17-year-old). They must be motivated by short-term contests.

We "max out" on all our lifts and "test" our speed and leaping abilities once a month. This inner squad competition is fierce but beneficial. We have a spring fling in April when we rent out a local health club, order pizza, and choose teams and have tournaments in various sports. This is something the players really look forward to.

Our promising juniors get to go to a scouting combine for our state in May to compete against the clock with weights and against players from all over the state. We take our top lifters to a competition in late May, where they compete against several other schools. In June, we always take our team to a paintball war facility. We have a draft among coaches to pick the best "commandos," who may not necessarily be the best football players. Then we all have fun playing war for a whole day.

ENCOURAGEMENT FOR A JOB WELL DONE.

The memories we make doing things like this are invaluable. Once summer comes, we go to several passing tournaments where we work on both passing and pass defense in a seven-on-seven (two-hand touch) environment. We always try to go out of our area to compete against the best in whatever we do. This gives our players a broader view of how good, or bad they are. Sometimes it can be humbling and other times it can be very exciting to go up against and defeat a big-name team.

We are constantly pushing our athletes to compete hard. I think this is a learned skill. We want to implant our competitive edge early, and push to perfect it in two-a-day drills. You cannot just train—you must give room for times of challenging and competing.

Motivation

The final factor in making what you have better is motivation. Every coach is probably a self-motivated person, which is probably one of the magic ingredients that keeps them coaching. So at times it may be difficult for some coaches to understand why their athletes need motivational "carrots" to keep them going. But young people, as a rule, are motivated by recognition and reward, which in reality is not so different from what motivates older people. Here's something we've discovered in the reward area: Our players will kill for a T-shirt!

Following is a quick list of recognition and reward motivators that have worked for us. You may want to adopt some of them or spin off from them to create some that fit the culture of your school and team:

The Bulletin Board

- We use charts for everything. They're a great tracking tool and are also terrific motivators.
- Our top lifters for each lift are posted on the board, and we also post a "top 20" in each lift.
- We have a "1200 Pound Club" with T-shirts. Athletes belong to this club when they've lifted accumulatively 1200 pounds in bench press, squats, cleans, and dead lifts.
- We keep "all-time-max" records that players can shoot for.
- We post anything positive about the sport or the players that gets printed in newspapers or magazines.
- Our top-notch game program features athletes who do well in the classroom. When they have achieved a 3.0-plus grade point average, we place their photos in the game program.
- We also print a picture of our 1200 pound club in the program.
- Offensive and defensive stats are tracked from year to year and go into our program as well.

Awards

- De-cleater Award—We get a local shoe store to sponsor an ad for our De-cleater Award winner (our best tackler) that features his photo.

- Pancake Award—A local pancake house sponsors an ad for our Pancake Award winner (our best blocker) with his photo.
- End of the Season Banquet—The big awards culminate at the banquet at the end of the season. We try to make this event as outstanding as possible. Many trophies are given for the usual categories, but we also have an award going to the best attitude (Coaches Award) and the best effort (Cougar Award), usually a scout team player.

Don't get me wrong—we push a total team theme as well, but anything we can do to kindle the fire under each individual will eventually help the TEAM reach its goals.

Part Six
Where the Rubber Meets the Road

Implementing Schemes, Evaluations & Drills

Chapter 19

Practice Schemes

*We're going to get two hours of good practice
even if it takes six hours.*
—Lou Holtz

One of the trends of recent times is to individualize offensive practice time. Players are kept separate to drill their various positions. This is done by almost everyone at any level. There is a definite need for individual, position-oriented drilling but not to the point of detracting or de-emphasizing the offense working as a whole.

You can specialize your squad to death. You must never drill for the sake of drilling. Each time you do anything in practice, it must have a direct correlation to actual football action. Whether it is a drill to teach aggressiveness, or simply to condition players, the coach must know that everything he does is enhancing the total picture.

The time factor must be taken into consideration when planning the week. I am not talking about summer training. I want to deal with the time you have between playing on Friday or Saturday and the next week's game. I will talk through a typical week for us. By seeing our schedule you should be able to detect definite emphasis on certain area.

The Typical Week: Friday to Friday

After a game, the coaching staff will meet to review the game. We want a clear picture of what really happened. Sometimes we spend all night and part of Saturday morning going over and over each play. We often will chart our drives and recheck the statistics.

On Saturday and Sunday, the individual coordinators for offense, defense, and special teams will review the game again, making notes for each player. They will also plan the attack for the next game based on what they have seen scouting, either live or on film. They will also refer to the scouting report that was put together the previous week. We then meet on Sunday night to coordinate everything and plan the coming week.

Monday: Review, Preparation, Light Practice

On Monday, the coaches and players will go over the scouting report during the lunch break. After school but before practice, the team meets with two important objective in mind:

1. to review the last week's game and
2. chalk and talk through the next opponent.

Any handouts such as new plays or adjustments are given out at this time.

Practice is in shells—helmets, shoulder pads, and shorts. It is a brisk walk through offense and defense. The only special team practice is the place kicker doing point after touchdown and field goal work. Our conditioning is fairly light, emphasizing running the soreness out on a long sustained jog.

Tuesday: Let's Go to the Video

Our Tuesday lunch meeting involves seeing the upcoming opponent on video. After school, the players dress from the hips down and lift weights in brisk 30-45 minute circuit workouts. We emphasize bench press, squats, cleans, and straight leg dead lifts, as well as neck and stomach work.

Practice includes stretching agility and team blocking-sled work. Since all our athletes, even the quarterback, are called on to block, we believe team sled work is a logical way to get everyone involved. Next, we work in individual offensive groups for 15-25 minutes. Here we fix whatever we thought was lacking in our last game. After that, we go into total offense. The usual progression is running plays against air, then versus blocking bags, then against live competition. We have our defense use small forearm "lobster" pads. This gives them protection from the constant pounding, but allows them full mobility in order to react and pursue the way a normal defense would.

MAKING THE COMPLEX SIMPLE.

When we go live, it is for only a short period. We believe live action is necessary to get the timing we need, but we do not want to leave our game on the practice field and be used up as early as Tuesday. We do stress using the whole time between whistles, and we purposely delay the whistle. This is where you can really push for the "off the film" blocking. If a player quits early, we really jump in his face. They must take pride in going hard the whole time.

We also push our backs to run as if they are going to score every time they touch the ball. We will set a cone or landmark 30-40 yards down field, and they must get there every time they run, whether it is against air, bags, or live—unless they get tackled. We often move the ball to simulate real drives. It gets the players accustomed to a game situation. We also go all the way back if we turn the ball over.

This tactic emphasizes the pain of turnovers. We will practice our punt team intermittently, as well as field goals. There are times when practicing goal-line stances, that we insert 12, 13, up to 15 players on defense. This really boosts the offense's confidence!

After offense, we go team defense as well as punt return practice. Finally, we end with specialty work for our kickoff team. The conditioning drill we employ on Tuesday is "perfect play" (explained in detail in Chapter 22).

Coach's note: Many coaches abuse conditioning. Football is not a track event. Running laps will help you prepare to run laps. We believe that if you can keep to a practice schedule without wasting even a minute, and all the while emphasize full effort and total hustle, then you are conditioning your team throughout practice. Perfect play simulates real football. Football is a series of starts and stops. It is explosion in short bursts. We love this drill because it is mentally, as well as physically, challenging. Tuesday is our longest day. We start lifting at 3:40 P.M., and we end our perfect play drill sometimes as late as 7:30 P.M. As the season progresses, we shoot to get done as early as 6:00 P.M.

Wednesday: More Videos, Drills, Simulations

On Wednesday, we again watch scouting videos at lunch. After school the players dress in full gear and get right to practice. After warm-ups, stretching, and team agility drills, we do some light tackle drills. These are often three-quarter speed form drills. We will go all out "live" tackling early in the season to see who can hit, but after that it is not necessary. We emphasize not leaving your feet and being athletic.

We work next on defensive individual time, often playing seven on seven (pass skeleton drill).

Total defense is next, which also simulates game situations. We will insert punt return and point after touchdown blocking teams. Next is total offense, along with going over goal-line and point after touchdown work. The special teams work will be kick return situations. We will condition with a defensive pursuit drill that emphasizes finding and attacking the ball.

Thursday: Dress Practice

Thursday lunch periods are free time. After school, the players dress in game jerseys and pants as well as helmets. They do a weightlifting circuit following a similar routine from the previous Tuesday. The emphasis is on a few quick reps and sets. By having our athletes lift two days a week, we believe we can help them maintain and gain strength throughout the season, and the team also keeps its edge as far as explosive power goes.

Maintaining flexibility also cuts down on the chance of injuries. We begin practice with a game called corner lob, which is fun and purposeful at the same time. Usually a coach will compete against a quarterback in throwing to various receivers, including linemen, who try to beat a defender to the corner of the end zone and catch a "touchdown."

On Thursday, we also simulate pregame entrance and do stretching exercises. The attitude is definitely lighthearted. We do one jumping jack and one push-up exercise. We even have a "nice day stretch" in which our captains instruct the team to get on their backs. Subsequently, a captain will shout out "nice day, isn't it?" The team, in turn, replies with various responses.

The players should enjoy Thursdays because they have worked hard Monday through Wednesday. They need to feel a sense of confidence because they have done their homework. The fine line between relaxed confidence and foolish horseplay can be controlled by the coach.

Next, we run through all our special teams, making sure we count eleven players each time. We check to see if our substitutes are ready and informed; go through our defensive sets, stunts, and blitzing schemes; and go over situations one more time. Finally, we run through our offensive plays quickly and discuss possible defensive adjustments and how to counter them.

All of this takes about an hour. It is not time to teach something new or to jump all over a player; it is time to reinforce previous learning and to set a calm, confident mood.

Coach's note: We have our players dress in game uniforms for three basic reasons:

1. to help put the players in a game-like state of mind,
2. to make sure the players have their uniforms, and
3. to see if they have washed their uniforms so they'll be clean for the beginning of the game.

This may sound trivial, but there are a lot of 16- and 17-year-olds who would forget their entire uniforms if they were not reminded.

Game Night

Because our games are usually on Friday nights, we give the players a few hours to collect their stuff after school or go home and relax. Usually about 4:00 P.M., we will meet at a restaurant in town and have a team meal. (We eat on the road if it is an away game.) After that, we will meet at the field and watch the first half of our junior varsity game. At half time, we go into the locker room and begin taping and dressing.

Finally, it is game time! We never warm up at the field or stadium where the game is to be played. This may seem unusual, but we always use an outside practice area for several reasons. One, we hate the nervousness of trying to look good in pre-game. We have never yet won a pre-game. Two, we do not want to let our opponents see us. Even though they may have scouted a number of games already, there is something about the pre-game that allows you to size up "your opponent."

We enjoy making a dramatic last-second appearance right before kick-off. It really builds anticipation both for the crowd and players to have to wait for our entrance. It is just another pride thing. At times, we have been penalized for delay of game for this tactic but have used that as a plus. It gives them an "us against the world" feeling. It is not unlike a boxer coming out late to a fight. Every moment helps build tension.

During the game, especially after the first series, we check with each offensive player to see how the other team is playing us. A good press box crew helps tremendously. Once we figure the opponent's scheme, we will adjust to attack it, realizing that just as we can change many times throughout the game, so can they. Remember to have the offense run the ball toward your sideline so you can get a better view.

After the game we check for injuries, and have a short team meeting. We then check stats and debrief as a coaching staff. We will finally grab something to eat and head out for our "night owl" coach's meeting and start the process all over again.

Chapter 20

Post Game: Evaluation of Your Offense

The will to win is meaningless without the will to prepare!"
—Joe Gibbs

To effectively evaluate the production of our offense, we scrutinize everything. We want measurable results that will show us for certain how we are doing in each area. If "it's broke," we want to fix it. If "it's working," we want to exploit it.

In this chapter, I will give examples of how we chart out the following post-game information:

- Game Drives
- Formation-Play
- Individual Offense
- Individual Mistakes
- Individual Praise
- Coaching Error and Adjustments
- Personnel Adjustments
- Play or Formation Adjustment
- Individual Drill by Position

We strive to aim for the goals we've all agreed upon, so we need to focus on specifics. Each week we want to see increased productivity by tightening up the machine and keeping it rolling.

By breaking information into manipulative pieces, we can get a handle on exactly what happened in a game. But the main question we always want answered is—what stopped us?

In going over these charts and notes, we can isolate exactly what strategy needs adjusting. They will become a valuable tool that will help you and your team to stay focused, which is one of the most important steps in building a winning team.

The players' names in the charts have, of course, been changed, but the sample information should be helpful. You can use the format of the charts as is or adapt them to fit your own needs.

Game Drive Chart

Game #6

The Drive Chart tells us the bottom line. Did we score?

We should expect to score on at least fifty percent of our drives.

Foothill			*Opponent*		
Yard line	# of plays	Result	Yard line	# of plays	Result
32	1	Int.	34	3	Punt
25	3	Punt	35	3	Punt
25	10	Downs	25	9	Downs
45	5	Downs	37	5	Int.
42	4	Downs	16	3	Punt
opp.29	2	TD	21	3	Punt
opp.49	3	TD	20	3	Punt
40	1	Half	25	2	Int.
27	4	Fumble	25	6	Punt
40	5	TD	31	4	Punt
45	4	TD	28	3	Punt
25	3	Punt	15	4	Punt
42	5	Punt	5	3	Punt
25	3	Punt			
opp.42	2	End Game			

Total
15 drives
4 TD's
4 Punts
3 Downs
2 Turnovers
2 Time

55 off. Plays

Total
13 Drives
0 TD's
10 Punts
1 Down
2 Turnovers

51 off. Plays

Formation-Play Chart

The Formation-Play Chart tells us what
specific set or play was effective.

Over the years, we try to keep track of what formation or plays work verses certain defenses. You will notice that the green and black (wings on) formation plays were the most effective. This was because the defense was loaded up into the single layer front mentioned previously.

Pro Right
30 Cut = 3 yards
24 Toss = 2 yds.

Pro Left
25 Boot Pass = Inc.
62 Slant = Inc.

Twins Left
61 (pass) = Inc.

Tight Right
28 Pitch Sweep = 10 yds
24 Toss = 5 yds, 2 yds
25 Trap = 4 yds, 1 yd
25 Trap Pass = Inc.

Tight Left
29 Pitch Sweep = 3 yds
25 Toss = 1 yd
24 Trap = 18 yds

Double Wing (Regular)
45 Toss = Fumble, -1 yd
24 Reverse = 16 yds, 43 yds
31 Cut = 6 yds
28 Pitch Sweep = 1 yd
45 X-Toss Pass = Inc.
24 Toss = 2 yds
49 Sweep = 2 yds
31 Dive = 1 yd
19 Scissors Pass = Inc.

Double Wing (W) Black or Green Set
45 Toss = 27, 25, 8, 7, 2, 12, 8
24 Toss = 3, 7, 5, 19, -4, 27, 24
30 Cut = 3, 2
45 Reverse = 33, 45, 20
24 Reverse = 8
31 Dive = 2
19 Keep = 2

Total
375 Rushing
40 Passing
415 Total

Individual Offense Chart

The Individual Offense Chart tells us who has the hot hand.

Who should be getting more carries?

Running Backs

Name	Carries	Yds.	Ave.	TD's
Butchman	11	67	6.0	1
Ingers	9	50	5.5	2
Yount	13	77	5.9	1
Stalls	18	165	9.1	1
Storm	1	8	8	0
Garry	1	-4	-4	0
Traps	1	2	1	0
Groaden	1	2	1	0
Mageski	4	11	2.8	0

Note: We chart all other areas as well but our main focus—and the focus of this book—is what strides we make on the ground, because if our running game is shut down, nothing else will matter!

Individual Mistake Chart

Fixing what's broke.

The mistake chart is announced to the players right before we watch the film of the previous game. We want to work on fixing flaws throughout the next week to avoid turning blunders into habits.

O LINE

Players #	Position	Note on Errors
56	RG	Hit air (i.e. missed block) X3
		Must seal block better on scissors pass
		See D.L. # on pre-snap read
		Go up field sooner on pitch sweep
58	RT	Why cup block on 60 series pass?
		Stop holding (tackled the LB)
	Tight End	
81	RTE	Get inside LB Vs DBL eagle defense
		Fight for ball when poorly thrown
		Stay on bear crawl longer on "Scoop Block"
	Running Back	
31	Rwing	See hole to the inside on reverse
		Go outside move on pitch sweep
		Too many cuts!—get up field
	Quarterback	
8	starting QB	Poor pitch (too high) on toss
		Overthrew X3 (get your feet set)
		Roll out wider on scissors pass

Praise Charts

The Praise Chart documents who is doing it right.

We give out awards on Monday—anything from T-shirts to candy bars—for good effort and great play to those who have earned it.

I. ***Pancakes*** (i.e. knock down blocks)

Players #	# of knockdowns	
50	3	
04	2	**Total Team Pancakes**
65	1	
80	4	10

II. ***Super Effort***

Player	Pos.	Note
Ramirez	center	3 pancakes, very efficient, super DBL teams
Jones	TE	3 catches, 2 pancakes, super scoop blocks

III. ***Awards*** (players of the game)

Overall best	=	**Smith** (80 yards on offense, 10 tackles defense)
Special team	=	**James** (blocked a punt)
Best special unit	=	**Kickoff** (kept inside 30, recovered on side)

Coaching Error Notes

I have found the Coaching Error notes invaluable.

There is nothing worse than making repeated coaching errors.

1. Check on inexperienced replacement sooner (Johnson at left tackle hurt our running game—should have pulled him.)
2. Should have adjusted to Green and Black scheme (wings on) sooner—did not adjust until 3rd QTR.
3. Don't give up on play action passes so soon—should have done more vs. loaded front.
4. Use X-toss and reverse vs. over aggressive defense.
5. Get on refs about D-line tackling our pulling linemen.

Personnel Adjustments

Personnel changes or movement help us also in our production process.

1. Rest Mathews at right tackle for 2 weeks—ankle.
2. Get Stalls more carries—very effective!
3. Take Wells off rotation of TE's—he cannot block.

Formation/Play Adjustments

Whole team concepts

Notes on formation remind us through next week to introduce, cancel, or change certain formations—while helping us to become more potent.

I-Pro Rt/Lft
—Introduce weak side toss

I-Twins
—Adjust crack back angle on sweep

I-Trips
—Reteach alignment checks to avoid penalties

Double wing
—Toss blocking must be adjusted by checking DE, CB location.
—Talk about single blocking OT, allowing TE to block LB.

I-Pro
—Adjust tailback depth on trap.

Individual Drill Chart by Position

We have to simultaneously balance fixing the problems of last week and preparing for the opponent this week.

The individual drill charts help each position coach because it gives each one a specific focus on what to do next.

RB & QB—Coach Smith
- wings down blocks (sustain)
- FB pre-snap reads kickout DE or CB
- QB fakes (demand excellent fake—no ball drill)

TE—Coach Jones
- scoop block technique vs. DE on sweeps
- fight on L.O.S. to get into pattern quicker

O-line—Coach Elkins
- head position on 7 technique
- "Frog Tunnel Drill"—to pull better vs. D line who grab ankles
- Cut Drill—guards must read on the run better
- Center back side seal blocks (keep feet, turn body)

Individual Drill Chart by Position

We have to simultaneously balance fixing the problems of last week and preparing for the opponent this week.

The individual drill charts help each position coach because it gives each one a specific focus on what to do next.

RB & QB—Coach Smith
- wings down blocks (sustain)
- FB pre-snap reads kickout DE or CB
- QB fakes (demand excellent fake—no ball drill)

TE—Coach Jones
- scoop block technique vs. DE on sweeps
- fight on L.O.S. to get into pattern quicker

O-line—Coach Elkins
- head position on 7 technique
- "Frog Tunnel Drill"—to pull better vs. D line who grab ankles
- Cut Drill—guards must read on the run better
- Center back side seal blocks (keep feet, turn body)

Chapter 21

DRILLS

*Don't mistake activity for achievement—
practice it the right way.*
—John Wooden

This entire chapter focuses on drills that will prepare your athletes to be more effective in this specific attack.

Everything we do during our practice has a purpose. A football specific movement should be incorporated into each drill you use. Too much practice time can easily be wasted on useless and senseless drills. We also design practice so players will be on the move from start to finish. For example, you should be able to get through 3-4 different drills in a 15-minute period. You won't need hours of "conditioning" at the end of your practice if you demand full hustle on all drills and spend practice time practicing instead of talking.

Offensive Line Agility Drills

Our first set of drills is for agility work. We also use these to warm up. Have players form four lines of equal number; preferably with guards in the two inside lines and tackles in the two outside. The outside arm of each player should be down. The coach should be standing 10 yards away (Diagram 21-1). The first thing we do is our get-offs. Which is just a 10 yard sprint, work on explosion and quick feet. Next is our angle sprint. We want our players to step at a 45° angle using their outside foot. The step should be between six and twelve inches. This will assist them in down blocking on linebacker cut-off blocks.

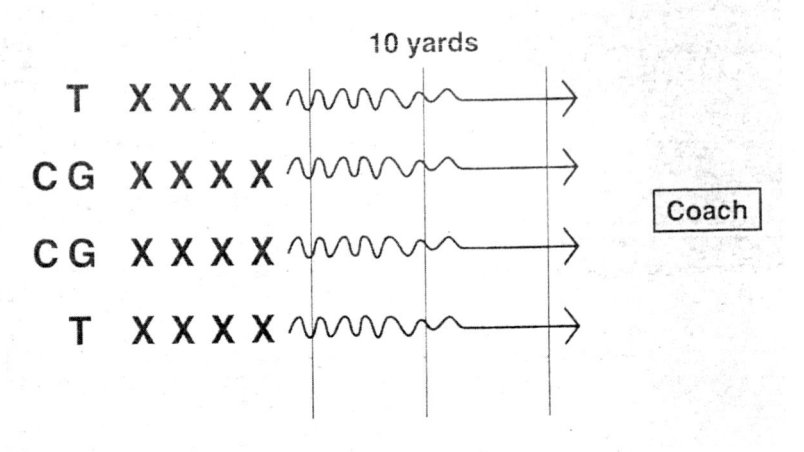

```
                    10 yards
    T   X X X X ～～～～→
    
    C G X X X X ～～～～→
                                              Coach
    C G X X X X ～～～～→
    
    T   X X X X ～～～～→
```

DIAGRAM 21-1   AGILITY DRILLS

After that, we have the players practice pulling. The two lines to your right pull left, and the left two pull right. The tackle should cut up after about five yards, or you can put out cones for a more specific marker. Emphasize throwing the outside arm to open the body. Also have them rotate and step with their outside foot. This will increase the speed of their pull.

Another important point is changing from the horizontal pull to the vertical down field attack. They must not round the corner. Push them to plant and accelerate.

Next we will P.P. block. They should dive out on their bellies as far as possible, bear crawl to the five yard stripe, then get up and sprint the next five.

Aggressive blocking drills are next. Have the players step forward hard and low to sell the run then back up with their feet moving quickly in small steps. Make sure they are cocked, low and in a good football position. After a couple of seconds of running in place yell, "cover!" They should then sprint 10 yards to simulate a down field block after the ball is released.

TECHNIQUE, TECHNIQUE, TECHNIQUE!

The last technique is the pivot block, which starts the same as "aggressive," but ends with the entire line rotating 45° in unison. They should then sprint on the "cover" command.

Z-Series Drills

When working on body mechanics or positioning skills, we will have our athletes do the next series of drills. The football position or "fit" position is the blocking stance the linemen should assume just before contact in an aggressive pass block. The legs should have a definite "Z" bend. The head should be up, eyes level. The chest out, and the back arched. The hands locked out front. We will do a "30 second" drill to practice holding this position. This is a great training method early on when reteaching players in spring ball.

After this, we will do our leap frog drill. Starting with the same stance described previously, we will then rotate our arms back and leap as high and as far as we can utilizing our leg explosion and arm thrust. The goal is to try to cover 10 yards using as few as three jumps.

Since we don't actually use cup blocking we don't have many pass blocking drills. We do, however, have an "aggressive" pass blocking series we call Z-Series. Using the "fit" position, the offender will back peddle while the defender will run forward in a zigzag motion, trying to outflank the block. The blocker will rotate his hips to stay in front. The blocker must give ground grudgingly, little by little. We do this in three parts. Take a look at Diagram 21-2, "Z Series."

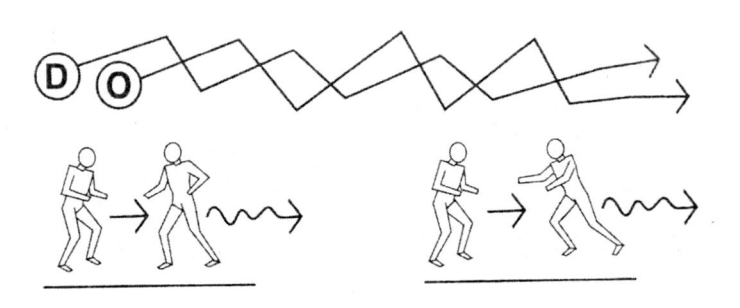

DIAGRAM 21-2 Z-SERIES

Part one is "Z-off" where the offensive lineman holds his hands behind his back and works to stay in front without making contact. This is a movement drill. Part two is the "Z-on" or "blind-Z." In this drill we do the same as "Z-off," but place our face mask on the defender's chest. This allows for the "feel" of the defender. This works on anticipating the next move by determining if the defender lunges right or left. The blind part is where you have the offensive linemen close their eyes. This is an advanced technique and young players will not be very successful at the start.

The last part is "Z-hands" or "Z-live." The hands are now locked into the chest and are used to feel, steer, and catch the opponent. This is an excellent drill to teach arm control. With today's rules freeing the linemen to utilize their arms, it is imperative that they be drilled and encouraged to use them. The "live" part comes by allowing the defender to use "anything" he can to get free, which includes even illegal techniques that will be seen in a game. The offender must work on quick recovery and balance.

For more arm work we have a whole series of drills to instill quick reaction and proper placement. My personal favorite is called "quick draw." Place two linemen face to face with their arms down to their sides. On the whistle they should bring their hands (thumbs together) up into the chest of the opponent. They should attempt to lock the arms at the elbow. The goal is to be the first one to get your hands inside in order to gain control. Off of this we will work on the "draw & drive" drill. This is the same as "quick draw," but at the point of contact, the linemen should drop their hips into "fit" position and shove up and back, taking little steps to drive the opponent back past the chalk line they are standing on. The winner will be easily spotted. Emphasize being quick, getting low, and driving hard.

Sled Drills: 6-Point Progression

Sled work is invaluable to any running team. We spend hours, especially in pre-season, on our five- or seven-man "buddy." We start with our six- point progression drill—two hands, two knees, two feet (Diagram 21-3). The idea is to teach hip rotation and proper angle of explosion. On the designated snap count, the linemen should push off with their hands and toes, forcing their shoulders into the sled's pad. They should end up with their eyes up, their shoulder and forearms ripping into the pad, and their hips rolled down (crotch in the dirt). Also, they should have proper width between their feet.

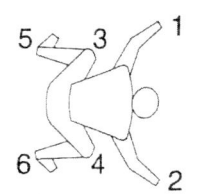

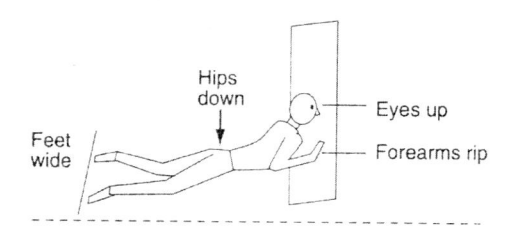

21-3 6-POINT PROGRESSION

Teach an "up and through" angle of explosion. Do this for both shoulders. Then do the same drill from a three-point stance. We will then drive the sled up and down the field until we feel we have enough "gas in the tank." Practice blocking must be more difficult than games. We even do a no-huddle drill, especially with our starting line. I'll yell "no-huddle," reset them, and have them drive for four or five snaps. The toss offense demands moving people play after play. It must be simulated on the sled daily.

Live Progression Drills

We will do the same type of progression with a live partner. We will lock players at the shoulders and practice hip rotation and "root hog" techniques. Players should work to get "low pad" and drive in small increments using hands and toes. See Diagram 21-4, "Live Progression." Next, we will go to the three point stance and drive. You can tell who wins by which side of the line you end up on. We will then separate the two players by six inches and get into the "live" portion of the drill.

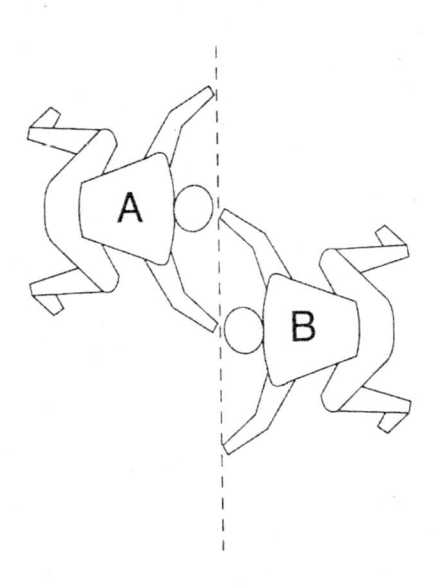

21-4 LIVE PROGRESSION

Combination Drills

Actual technique blocking can be simulated with our combination drills. These drills can be done with tight ends. You can do several drills at the same time, utilizing all your linemen. The first one is our double-team work (Diagram 21-5A). Second is our "chip" blocking work off of our doubles (Diagram 21-5B). If the driver feels his post-man can finish the block, he can release (chip off) and catch pursuing defenders.

Another exercise using the same set-up is the "half-man blitz block." The post-man uses an arm and shoulder on the defensive lineman, but can still utilize his other half to stop (or at least slow up) blitzing linebackers. Stress using the flipper—forearm and elbow—so as not to commit a holding violation.

Next, we work down blocking with a half line set-up, as shown in Diagram 21-5C. The defenders should try to charge across the line to beat the angle. The offenders should aim their heads in front of their charge. They also should utilize the 45° angle step technique. Be slow to blow the whistle on this one. Create a killer instinct by forcing the offensive linemen to finish their blocks. Make them drive the man 10-15 yards before stopping the drill.

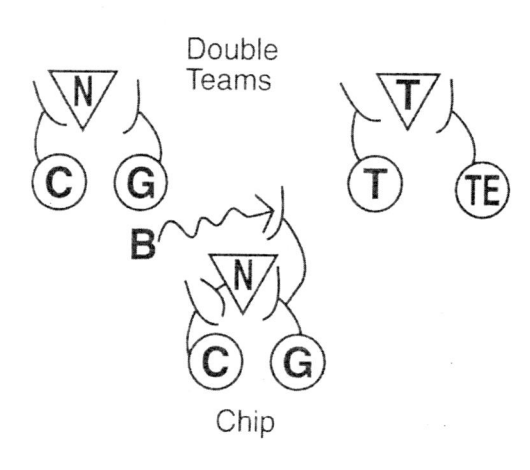

Double Teams

Chip

21-5A COMBO DRILLS

←— Blitz —→

½ Man

- inside postman catches blitz

21-5B COMBO DRILLS

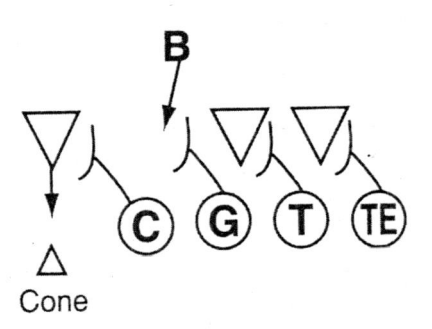

Cone

Down blocking

21-5C COMBO DRILLS

Log-Block Drills

This brings us to the next step in the series: *log blocking* (Diagram 21-6). Again, this works on finishing blocks. We have a runner skim by the defender. When the defender reaches for the runner, the offensive player should really attack up and under in order to level him to his back (pancake him).

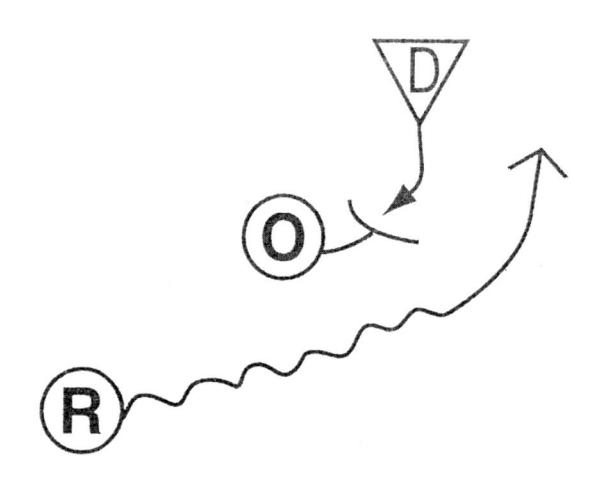

21-6 LOG BLOCKING
Note: AS THE DEFENDER REACHES FOR THE RUNNER, THE OFFENSIVE LINEMAN SHOULD DIG UNDERNEATH THE EXTENDED ARM AND "ROLL" HIM (PANCAKE) ONTO HIS BACK.

Bag Series Drills

To simulate other plays, we do our bag series. (Diagram 21-7 series). You can come up with "play-like drills" very easily. We practice toss, sweep, cut, cross toss (reverse), all using cones and blocking shields. This allows for speed and timing, but without the bumps and bruises of live play. Have the defenders act like live players. In toss (Diagram 21-7A), the backers should fly to the ball. In sweep (Diagram 21-7B), the corner should take an inside route, then switch up and fight to the outside. The guards should adjust. In the cut (Diagram 21-7C), the defensive tackle should at times stay on the line of scrimmage,. but then other times should penetrate deep. The guard should not waste a block on the latter, but go get the corner back. In the cross toss or reverse drill (Diagram 21-7D), the defensive end should do the same as the defensive tackle, giving different looks.

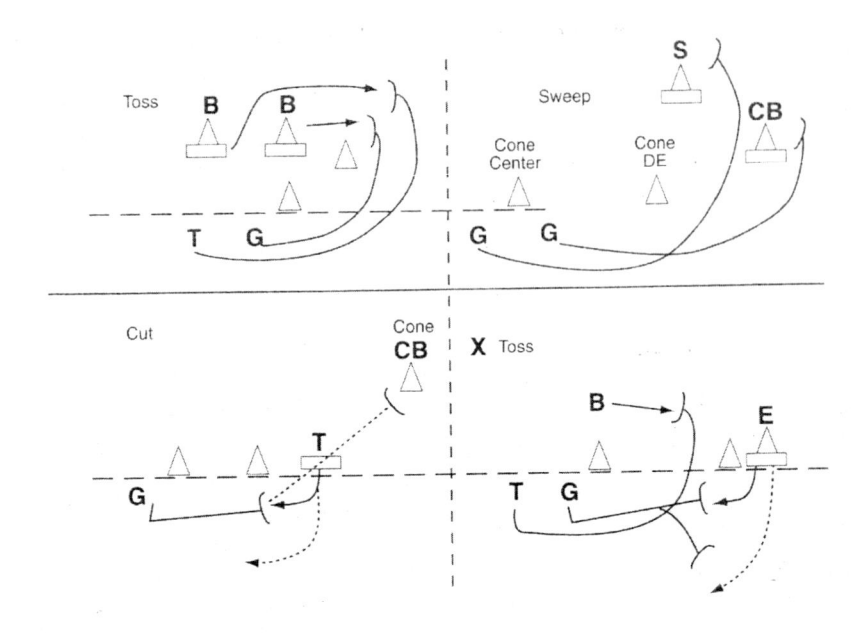

21-7 BAG SERIES [21-7A TOSS 21-7B SWEEP 21-7C CUT 21-7D X-TOSS]

Down and Dirty Drills

For teaching aggressiveness or just having fun, these drills are terrific (Diagram 21-8 series). To really give our guys the feeling of what it's like to de-cleat someone, we have the splatter drill (Diagram 21-8A). We have a live dummy stand in front of a high jump pit. He can cross his arms, or even hold a blocking shield to protect himself. The other guy gets a five-yard start. His goal is to accelerate and explode up and through the "dummy." This creates hunger for contact. It is also a good teaching method for explosion angles.

Another aggressive drill is the towel drill (Diagram 21-8B). We have two guys stand face-to-face, each holding onto a towel with both hands. The object is to get the towel away from your opponent.

To teach leverage, we use the sumo circle (Diagram 21-8C). We basically do the same thing as the sumo wrestlers. The object is to move your opponent out of the circle. Usually the low man wins, just as in football.

The anything goes fumble drill (Diagram 21-8D) is another super way to let your hair down and see who your fighters are. The coach tosses out the ball and two guys go and try to bring it back.

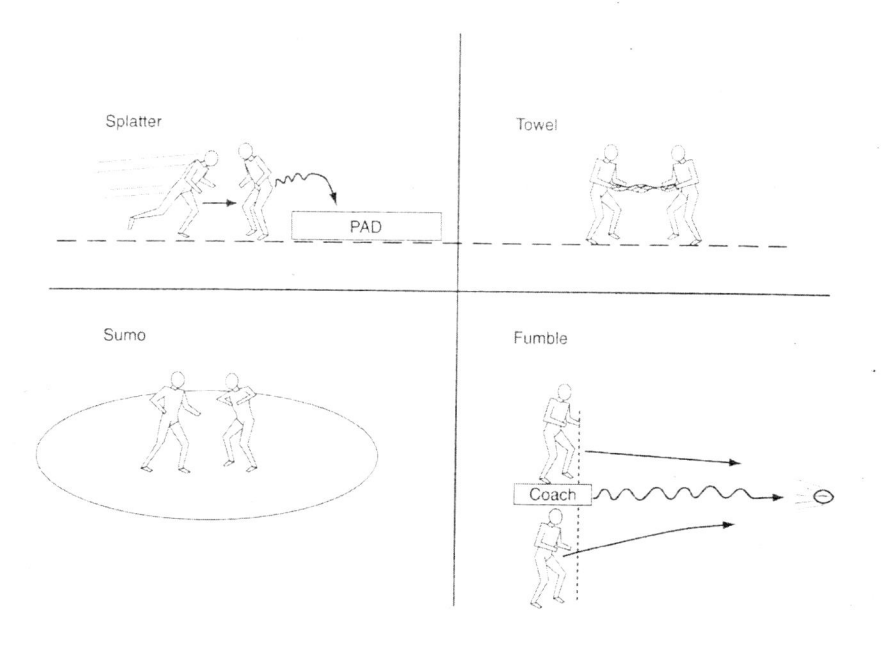

21-8 DOWN AND DIRTY DRILLS
[21-8A SPLATTER 21-8B TOWEL 21-8C SUMO 21-8D FUMBLE]
Note: OBVIOUSLY YOU HAVE TO WATCH THESE DRILLS CLOSELY—USING GOOD JUDGMENT AS TO THE SAFETY OF YOUR PLAYERS.

One-on-One Drills

The one-on-one drills (Diagram 21-9) round out the selection. The first part pits two offenders against each other. The object is to drive block each other back across the line. The next is the aggressive pass block drill. The offender must block the defender and keep the defender in front of him for three seconds. The key is to recover from the opponent's first move; that is, a swim, rip, and so on.

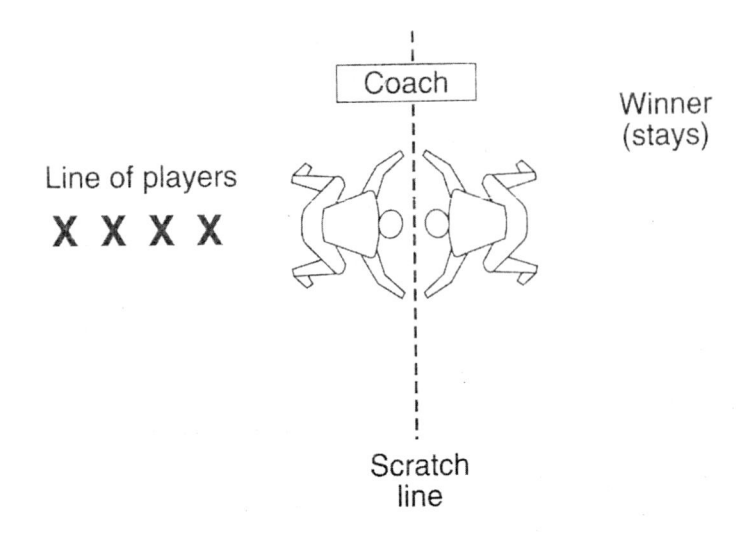

```
            Coach
Line of players          Winner
                         (stays)
X X X X

            Scratch
            line
```

21-9 ONE-ON-ONE

You can run these drills by rotating in new people each drill, or by having the winner stay on the field up to three times, or the winner stays until he gets beat. This is a great way to find out who your dominant blockers are in both run and pass techniques.

Additional Quarterback and Running Back Drills

In the following pages you will find several extremely useful drills to help your players better develop their skills. Each drill is designed for the exact action they will use in this offense and also to simulate game action situations.

Lane Drill (21-10)

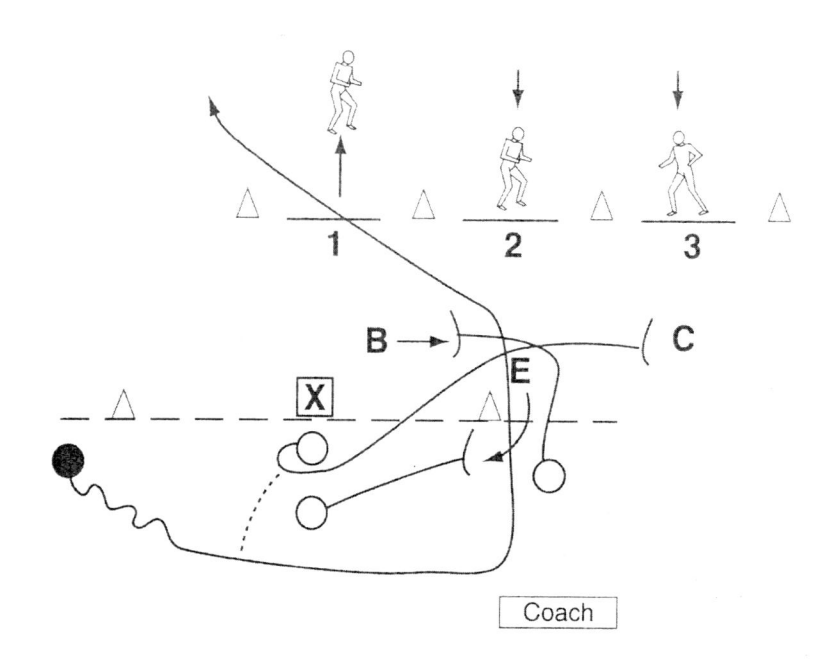

Equipment: Six cones, footballs

Personnel: Center, quarterback, fullback, wings
Scout linebackers, defensive end, fillers

Drill Action: The coach stands behind the offense and holds up one, two, or three fingers to indicate which lane to leave open. On the snap of the ball, two fillers (who were not called) step up to fill the gap while the number called backs away. The fullback, onside wing and quarterback work on their toss blocks. The called wing should get the pitch, plant, and as he's attacking the line, check to see which lane is open and attack it accordingly.

178 Chapter 21

Fake Drill (21-11)

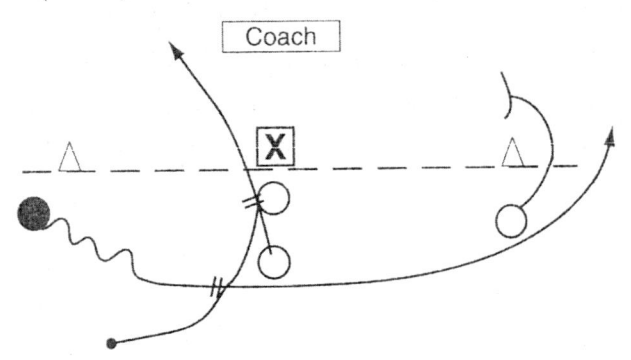

Equipment: Two cones

Personnel: Wings, fullback, quarterback

Drill action: The unit will carry out cut, sweep, and scissors pass action both left and right. Since these plays always look the same, this drill helps develop perfect faking action. No football is used because it helps to emphasize deceptive techniques. All fakes should be carried out for a full 10 yards. The quarterback should always fake a realistic throwing action.

Timing Drill (21-12)

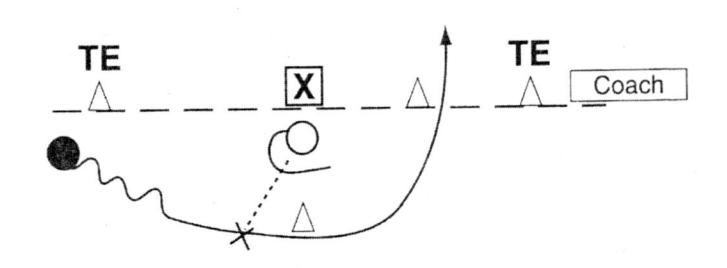

DRILLS 179

Equipment:	Four cones, footballs, stopwatch
Personnel:	Centers, quarterback, wings
Drill Action:	The coach stands just beyond the cones on the line with a stopwatch. The quarterback and wing go through toss action. The wing should be timed from the time he gets the ball to the time he crosses the line. The optimum time is in 1.3 seconds. Note: The cone behind the center is approximately five yards deep.

Sweep Drill (21-13)

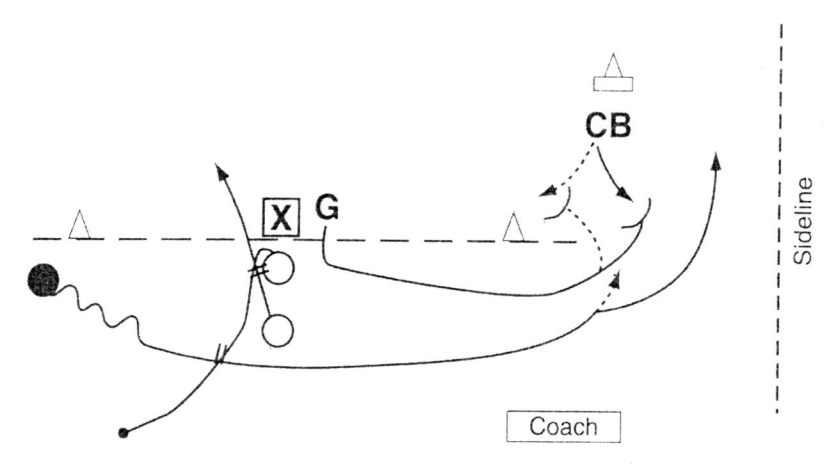

Equipment:	Two cones, footballs, one shield
Personnel:	Wings, fullback, quarterback, center, guards, scout corner back
Drill Action:	The wing should get into the "wake" of the pulling guard. He should concentrate on his rear end. Once the corner back commits to his attack angle, and the guard is forced to take him in or out, the wing should make his cut the opposite way. The wing can also work to "set" the block with a good head fake.

Gauntlet Drill (21-14)

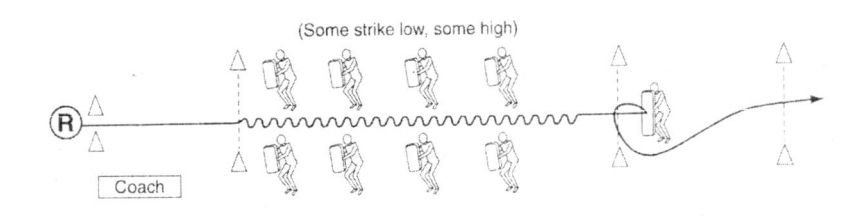

(Some strike low, some high)

Equipment:	Eight cones, eight shields, one blocking bag, footballs
Personnel:	All ball carrier types, nine bag holders
Drill Action:	The ball can be pitched, handed off, or given previous to take off. Once the ball carrier (R) takes off, he should try to reach full speed before entering the tunnel (10 yards). The runner should have two hands covering the ball and keep his knees pumping high. Once, or if, he gets through the tunnel, he should attack the big bag and work a spin move off of it, recover and sprint to the end. The bag holders will deliver a variety of blows both low and high. If the runner gets knocked down, he should get up immediately and continue until he is through. If he fumbles, he must be made to go again.

Chase Drill (21-15)

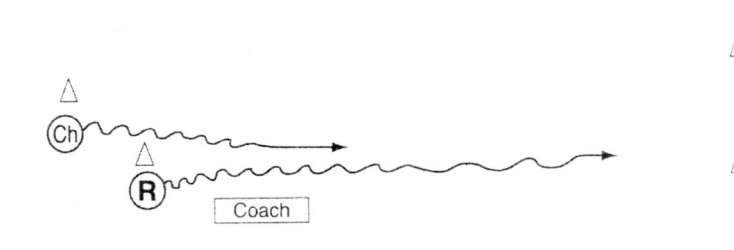

Equipment:	Three cones, footballs
Personnel:	All ball carriers, chasers
Drill Action:	Two players of equal speed run 40 yards. The chaser will start two to three yards behind the runner. The chaser can dive at the runner's feet—if he can't overtake him normally, attempting a "shoelace" tackle. The runner should work on his bursts to speed away from tacklers or his "high stepping" action if a "shoelace" is attempted.

Drag Drill (21-16)

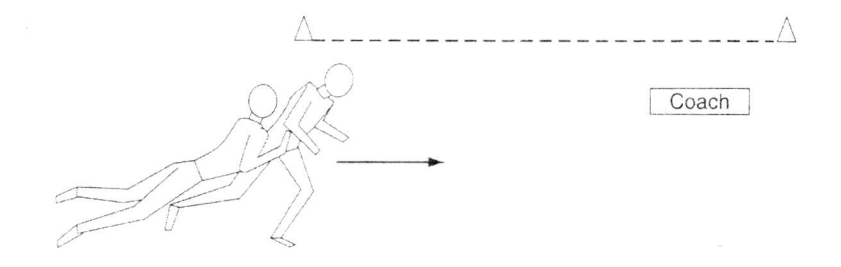

Equipment:	Two cones
Personnel:	All ball carriers, dragmen
Drill Action:	One player hangs onto the hips of another. The drag man lets his legs go limp to increase friction. The runner must lean forward and utilize good leg drive to carry (drag) his man 40 yards.

Chapter 22

BUYING INTO THE TOTAL PACKAGE

Individual commitment to a group effort—that is what makes a team work, a company work, a society work, a civilization work.
—Vince Lombardi

In an interview after he had dislocated his shoulder while tackling an opponent who had intercepted his pass, Football Hall of Famer Joe Namath was questioned about his reasons for trying to make the tackle and risking injury, to which he replied, "If you're not going to go all the way, why go at all?" This is how I feel when it comes to "The Toss" offense. You cannot "dabble" with "The Toss." It is something you must "go all the way with" in order to be successful.

The main reason is time. Unless you are in an extremely unusual situation, you do not have enough hours to run "The Toss" as part of another multi-faceted attack. Something will suffer. Whether it be your defense, your special teams, or your offensive efficiency. "The Toss" is predicated on ball control, and ball control comes from not hurting yourself with mental errors and turnovers, both of which occur when you have not spent hours of repetition on every single play.

In this chapter, I will discuss the way to implement the whole package. Again, remember this warning: If you intend to use it as one of many additions to your play book, you will end up frustrated, and you will junk it because you have not taken the time to do it right, you really do not have faith in it.

Ball Control

Ball control is your best friend in this scheme because it can lead to multi-play drives where you eat the clock in big chunks. We have had drives that took up entire quarters. We do this with several techniques built into our scheme. First, we run the ball, and that takes time. Second, we take our time getting to the line of scrimmage. That's correct—we walk to the line. Former Ohio State Football Coach Woody Hayes might roll over in his grave, but we do not ask our boys to sprint out of the huddle. This comes from Don Markham's philosophy of putting effort where it is necessary—namely, between the whistles. Like Football Hall of Famer Earl Campbell, we might ramble for a great 40-yard breakaway with the speed of a jaguar, but we look like a train wreck when we slowly unpile, gather to the huddle, and finally get back to the line.

It is almost comical to watch, but the method to the madness is that we steal as much time as we can, and we fully recover between each play. We call this Blue or slowdown pace. We also have a Red, or a two-minute drill where we can go without a huddle or call two or three plays in a row, and we hustle the whole time. We practice both tempos all week. Sometimes we go Red just for a change of pace to throw the defense into a panic.

Your time on offense equals time spent on the field by your opponent's defense. It is a well known fact that is physically harder to play defense (where you must react) than it is to play offense. Our goal is to win the war of attrition. We do this by pounding the defense into submission. We want to wear them down with our double-teams, down blocks, stampedes, and kick-out blocks. We do this by spreading the wealth.

With two wings, a fullback, and a quarterback who can run, we believe our arsenal will never run dry. We are not tiring one back but attacking with four fresh ones. Add to this that we believe in two platoons, one offense and one defense, while most of our opponents have at least half of their team going both ways. You can see why defenses begin to cave in quickly. Also, by having a year-round commitment to weight lifting, we feel we get stronger as the season progresses, whereas most teams are doing the opposite.

Ball control demoralizes even a great defense. The better the defense, the longer it takes, but if you adhere to the principles and do not panic (that is, throw the ball too much), you will eventually take over the game.

Commitment to Perfection

The next part of the package ties into the fanatical dedication to perfection. We run what we call "perfection drill" where we run 400 yards of offense, in 10-yard increments, against air. We check *Everything*! If the offense makes one error—a dropped pass, offsides penalty, a missed conversion, and so on—we go all the way back to the goal-line and start the series over. For instance, if we get a perfect drive (100 yards) and fumble after 90 yards on the second drive, we go back 90 yards and start the drive over. Early in the year, the 400 yards takes 800 to 1200 yards, depending on the focus of attention that day.

Mistakes kill a football team. We believe and preach to our athletes that no one can stop us, except ourselves. For this reason, we spend hours making sure that we do not stop ourselves.

Turnovers are our nightmare. Because we do pitch the ball a high percentage of the time, we cannot afford a lack of focus at any point. If the wing coming in motion gets lazy mentally and begins looking at the hole before tucking the toss away, the ball is gone and we have just stopped our own drive.

We learned this painful lesson once near the end of a game. We had a small lead, and we were going in for a score that would clinch the victory. It was third down. We were on their 20-yard line, and we needed about four yard to go for a first down. At worst, we could turn the ball over on downs and play prevent defense. We called the toss play. The quarterback pitched the ball, but the wing looked away for a split second. The ball careened off his chest and fell to the ground where he subsequently kicked it while trying to gather it in. The ball bounced right into the corner back's hands—the corner back who happened to be the fastest guy on the field—and he ran the ball 90 yards for a touchdown. They kicked the extra point, and we went home with a loss. Perfection must be a priority.

The Four-Down Concept

Another concept is the four-down plan. We believe that we have four downs to get 10 yards. Most teams feel that three downs is the limit, and then it is time to punt. Our thinking is that we will always get at least three yards out of our toss play. We use the no play in time-out situations on third or fourth down. We also use the offbeat count or sneak on sound or silent freeze sneak. Depending on field position, we may or may not take a chance on the fourth-down play, but if we are inside the 40, we will go for it more often than not. This obviously puts the pressure on our defense if we fail, but since we base our attack on controlling the clock and winning with a small lead, we will take the chance.

Play Selection

Each coach has his own style when it comes to play selection. That is what makes coaching so enjoyable: The ability to stamp one's character onto an offensive attack that motivates many offensive coordinators. However, too many coaches base their play selection on preference rather than logic. A game plan must be based on the hard rock foundation of your entire scheme and not left to split-second guessing or the use of old favorites to dictate the call. Another common fault, especially of younger coaches, is a lack of patience. Without patience, you should not attempt to run this offense. Play selection has many variables, and I will not attempt to cover them all, but a few concepts or foundational rules will help.

Working "The Toss" Play

The first law of this scheme is "toss till you drop!" I've said this before, but I'll say it again: The toss is the center of all the other plays. You simply cannot expect to run any other play without developing your toss early in the game. We have had series in which we run the toss play almost exclusively. If it is working, why go away from it?

You must always keep in mind the fatigue factor. Champion boxer Rocky Marciano used to pound on the arms and shoulders of his opponents round after round until the middle of the fight or later when the opponent's beaten and exhausted limbs would become useless as a defense. He then would go in for the finishing blows to the head and body. In that style, "The Toss" does more than gain yards. With the mismatch of twice the blockers per defenders, it literally pummels the defense.

Once the toss play has been established, you are free to do a number of things, depending on the reaction of the defense and your team's particular skills. If you desire to throw the ball, do so on first down, or on second and short. Another good time is after a long run. All of these times have one thing in common: They are all running situations, which is when you want to use play action passes. Never throw when you're traditionally expected to throw!

Running Trick Plays

Trick plays are excellent after gaining respect for the toss. They are not risky when you run them at a time *when you do not have to!* Trick plays may be as mild as a simple cross-toss counter play or as wild as pitch pass or cut-option. These plays will break a game wide open if successful. And as long as you run them at the right time (after you have rocked the defense on its heels) and place (inside the opponent's side of the 50-yard line), then even it if flops, the most you lose is a down. But even then you implant a whole world of worries in the mind of the defense, which must now be aware of even more areas of attack.

These are only a few suggestions, but they cover the most common blunders of coaches who desire to run "The Toss" offense but pull the plug too early or try to be cute by "mixing it up." The "mixing" should come only on the tail of successful drives created by several toss plays.

Running "The Toss" to the Sideline

One quick coaching note as to which side to run the toss: Obviously, the greatest advantage to an even-up look (double tight end, double wing) is its symmetrical nature. We can run all plays exactly the same right and left. But early on, it is helpful to run the toss to your sideline. Especially to the short side. This allows you to see how it is developing. You get a fishbowl look at everything that is going on. Even the coaches in the press box can see better when the play is run near the sideline. Later on, if you are doing great and your fullback is knocking the socks off the defensive end, then it can be advantageous to run it to the opponent's sideline for intimidation purposes if for nothing else!

Scoring

A word on scoring would be appropriate here. Consider the time factor when thinking about the score. If you are controlling the clock, as you should, and your defense is playing at least adequately, then seven points is really closer to 14 points. Or, in other words, the spread between the leader and the loser is actually wider than the score indicates. With this in mind, you should value each scoring opportunity even more. If you get any chance to score, especially early in the game, take it. When it comes to choosing between a field goal and a touchdown, it is no contest. We will risk going on fourth down for the chance to get six points.

This comes from a strong confidence in our running game and the knowledge of the "double point" value mentioned earlier. Once we score, the next question is whether we go for a one- or two-point conversion. Again, if it is early, we want to widen the gap and put the opponent in a catch-up situation—so we will go for two until either we find that we are far enough ahead to "afford" to settle for one point or we run into a really tough goal-line defense.

Running Versus Passing

As far as run or pass inside the 10-yard line, the voice of Lou Holtz rings in my head. Although he is known as an innovator and an eclectic play caller, he preaches heavy about going with what got you there. If you have run over the defense for 80 yards, it seems ludicrous to risk giving up the ball and momentum by getting "tricky" with a pass.

ALWAYS LOOKING TO BREAK THE BIG ONE.

That is not to say we never pass on the goal-line, but we never, ever pass early in the game if our running games is successful.

To end this thought, I want to flip it over and speak about the effect on the opponent. If we are succeeding in our quest to chew up yards and the clock, and if we are up by 10 points or more, then we feel extremely confident that we have put the opponent into a state of panic. They must soon alter their game plan on both sides of the ball. On defense, they must adjust to stop the run or try using a blitzing scheme to disrupt the drive. On offense, they must begin thinking about scoring quickly, knowing the chances of getting the ball back in time to score twice and gain a lead is growing slimmer by the minute.

Of course, the way to score quickly is to throw the ball and throw it deep. Our defense just loves this. We have an aggressive, risk-taking defense. We rely on being sound in concept, but we are not above taking chances. We feel we can afford this because of our offensive productivity.

When we get a team in a catch-up, must-score position, look out! We usually rack up a lot of quarterback sacks. We also get close to three turnovers a game. Add to that the fact that our defense usually has several scores of its own after converting turnovers, and you can see why we love to see opponents get behind the score. Remember, our goal is to never give up the ball for any reason, and on the other end, we want to get as many "take-aways" as we can. This combination means lopsided scores in our favor.

Team Buy-In of the Plan

The last thing that merits mentioning when it comes to the total plan is selling it to your team. Good coaches exude confidence. Confidence comes from a knowledge that you have the best plan for your team. If you do not believe this, neither will they. However, if you do, then you must instill it into your players.

The feeling of confidence can be accomplished just by talking it up. Explain what you feel are the team's strengths. Explain your vision of success. Explain your level of expectation. Talk positive but be realistic at the same time. We try to tie our offensive philosophy into our program philosophy. We believe in:

1. outworking our opponents year round,
2. being unified by spending a lot of time working out, doing fund raising, and taking part in special events, and
3. having fun.

Football must be fun, or it is not worth doing.

With these as our base, we simply tie in our "smash mouth" offense as an extension of a simple, hard working, unified team that loves to have fun. We feel our offense fits in well.

Appendix

FROM THE BOOKS

If a coach can win consistently over a long period of time and continue to collect outstanding statistical achievements, we deem that coach and his system a winner. For this reason, I have included the following information. If, after reading this book, you still need proof that this offense can produce results, then this chapter should convince you.

Here is a history lesson of sorts taken right out of the California state record book. I have listed every statistic that you will need to measure a successful team and/or offense. It is a fine tribute to Don Markham because it shows his history as a coach with seven different high school teams since 1970, in which he took his teams to the section championship nine times and won five titles. It is also a tribute to his scheme, which he has so willingly shared with anybody who is interested. The following pages are just some of the amazing marks that this offense has achieved over the past 25 years.

It is also to be noted that most of the records are from teams that ran some sort of the I-formation Toss. The most recent phenomena of the Double Wing teams will be marked with a "D." Also, the records that were set by a Markham-coached team are designated with an "M."

I may have missed a few numbers, teams, or totals, but there is more than enough evidence here to show that this is the most prolific attack in high school, bar none!

California Records Set by High School Teams and Players Using the "Toss Style Offense"

State Placing	Most Points (Overall Season)	
1	880 Bloomington, 1994 (14-0) (1st also in Nation)	M,D
9	615 Foothill (Redding), 1993 (11-1)	D

State Placing	Most Points (Regular Season)	
1	646 Bloomington, 1994 (10-0) (2nd in Nation)	M,D
2	564 Foothill (Redding), 1993 (10-0) (11th in Nation)	D

State Placing	Highest Scoring Average (Overall Season)	
1	62.86 Bloomington, 1994 (14-0) (8th in Nation)	M,D
5	51.3 Foothill (Redding), 1993 (11-1)	D
7	51.00 Sepulveda LA Baptist, 1972 (9-1)	M

State Placing	Highest Scoring Average (Regular Season)	
1	64.5 Bloomington, 1994 (10-0)	M,D
4	56.4 Foothill (Redding), 1993 (10-0)	D

State Placing	Highest Point Differential (Overall Season)	
1	645 Bloomington, 1994 (14-0) (8th in Nation)	M,D
6	491 Foothill (Redding), 1993 (11-1)	D

State Placing	Highest Point Differential (Regular Season)	
1	526 Bloomington, 1994 (10-0)	M,D
2	462 Foothill (Redding), 1993 (10-0)	D

State Placing	Total Offense—Yards (Overall Season)	
3	6439 Bloomington, 1994 (14-0) (4th in Nation)	M,D

State Placing	Total Rushing—Yards (Overall Season)	
3	5568 Bloomington, 1994 (14-0) (4th in Nation)	M,D

State Placing	Total Offense Per Game (Yards)	
N/A	466.3 Bloomington, 1994 (14-0) (3rd in Nation)	M,D

State Placing	Rushing Average Per Game (Yards)	
N/A	401.5 Bloomington, 1994 (14-0) (6th in Nation)	M,D

Individual Records

State Placing	Most Touchdowns (Overall Season)	
1	46 David Dotson, Moreno Valley View, 1991 (11)	
2	45 Greg Oliver, Bloomington, 1994 (14)	M,D
18	36 Derek Sparks, Van Nuys Montclair Prep. 1989 (13)	

State Placing	Most Touchdowns (Regular Season)
1	44 David Dotson, Moreno Valley View, 1991 (10)
17	31 Derek Sparks, Van Nuys Montclair Prep. 1989 (10)

State Placing	Most Points (Overall Season)	
1	354 Greg Oliver, Bloomington, 1994 (14) (3rd in Nation)	M,D
2	282 David Dotson, Moreno Valley View, 1991 (11)	

State Placing	Most Points (Regular Season)
1	David Dotson, Moreno Valley View, 1991 (10)

State Placing	Most Touchdowns (Game)
8	David Dotson, Moreno Valley View, 1991 (56) vs Rim of the World (0), 1991

State Placing	Most Points (Game)
8	David Dotson, Moreno Valley View, 1991 (56) vs Rim of the World (0), 1991

State Placing	Most Touchdowns (Career)		
3	31	David Dotson, Moreno Valley View, 1989-91	

State Placing	Most 2-Point Conversions (Overall Season)		
1	41	Greg Oliver, Bloomington, 1994	M,D

State Placing	Most 2-Point Conversions (Regular Season)		
1	32	Greg Oliver, Bloomington, 1994	M,D

State Placing	Most Yards (Overall Season)		
1	3523	David Dotson, Morento Valley View, 1991 (11)	
4	2620	Ryan Knight, Riverside Rubidoux, 1983 (12)	
5	2576	Jeff Byrd, Garden Grove Rancho Alamitos, 1992 (14)	
9	2493	David Dotson, Moreno Valley View,. 1990 (10) jr	
11	2445	Craig Johnston, Whittier Christian, 1975 jr	
15	2380	Eleil Swinton, Van Nuys Montclair Prep., 1992 (13)	
16	2371	Steve Tretrick, Sepulueda, LA Baptist, 1972 (10)	M
17	2363	Ted Smith, Colton, 1974 (14)	
18	2391	Ramond Lee, Moreno Valley View, 1992 (12) jr	

State Placing	Most Yards (Regular Season)
1	David Dotson, Moreno Valley View, 1991 (10)
2	David Dotson, Moreno Valley View, 1990 (10) jr
3	Craig Johnston, Whittier Christian, 1975 (9)
10	Ryan Knight, Riverside Rubidoux, 1983 (9)
11	George Hemingway, Colton, 1986 (10)
18	Dana Riddle, Garden Grove Rancho Alamitos, 1989 (10)

State Placing	Most Yards (Game)	
1	507	David Dotson, Moreno Valley View (56) vs Rim of the World (0), 1991
2	501	Ryan Knight, Riverside Rubidoux (58) vs Corona (7), 1983
5	448	Craig Johnston, Whittier Christian (61) vs LA Baptist (6), 1975
7	445	David Dotson, Moreno Valley View (35) vs Riv. Norte Vista (3), 1991
8	431	David Dotson, Moreno Valley View (40) vs S.D. Montgomery (0), 1991

14   405   Ryan Knight, Riverside Rubidoux (38) vs Corona (39) 1982 jr

State Placing	Most Yards Career (Counting All Games)	
1	7257 David Dotson, Moreno Valley View, 1989-91 (31)	
3	5878 Eleil Swinton, Van Nuys Montclair Prep., 1990-92	
7	5213 Craig Johnston, Whittier Christian, 1973-75 (30)	
8	5181 Steve Tetrick, Sepuleuda, LA Baptist, 1970-72 (34)	M
13	4882 Eric Bieniemy, La Puente Bishop Amat., 1984-86 (35)	M
17	4597 Ryan Knight, Riverside Rubidoux, 1982-83 (23)	
19	4553 Marvin Williams, Colton, 1975-78	M

State Placing	Highest Yards-Per-Carry Average (Game)
4	47.7 Andrew Boesiger, Redding Foothill vs Oroville Las Plumbas (16) 1994 (143/3, 3 Tds)

State Placing	Most Yards Career (Counting Regular Season Only)	
1	David Dotson, Moreno Valley View, 1989-91 (30)	
2	Craig Johnston, Whittier Christian, 1973-75 (27)	
7	Eric Bieniemy, La Puente Bishop Amat., 1984-86 (29)	M

Individual Rushing Leaders of the Year (Overall Season)

1992	Jeff Byrd (Garden Grove, Rancho Alamitos): 2,576 yds (14 games)	
1991	David Dotson (Moreno Valley View): 3,523 yds (11 games)	
1989	Marshawn Thompson (La Puente, Bassett): 2,300 yds (12 games)	
1985	Richie Swinton (Van Nuys, Montclair Prep.): 2,231 yds (14 games)	
1984	Mark Ortega (La Habra, Whittier Christian): 2,044 yds (14 games)	
1983	Ryan Knight (Riverside Rubidoux): 2,260 yds (12 games)	
1978	Marvin Williams (Colton): 1,883 yds (13 games)	M
1975	Craig Johnston (Whittier Christian): 2,445 yds (9 games)	
1974	Ted Smith (Colton): 2,363 yds (14 games)	M
1972	Steve Tetrick (Sepuleuda, LA Baptist): 2,371 yds (10 games)	M

Individiual Rushing Leaders of the Year (Overall Season)

1992	Ramond Lee (Moreno Valley View): 1,920 yds (10 games) jr	
1991	David Dotson (Moreno Valley View): 3,345 yds (10 games)	
1990	David Dotson (Moreno Valley View): 2,493 yds (10 games) jr	
1989	Dana Riddle (G.G. Rancho Alamitos): 1,975 yds (10 games) jr	
1986	George Hemingway (Colton): 2,022 yds (10 games)	
1982	Ryan Knight (Riverside Rubidoux): 1,809 yds (10 games) jr	
1975	Craig Johnston (Whittier Christian): 2,445 yds (9 games)	
1972	Steve Tetrick (Sepuleuda, LA Baptist): 1,948 yds (8 games)	M

America's Highest Scoring Teams

Big Sandy, TX (1975)

43 Winoma 0
54 Sabine 0
66 Union Grove 0
55 Hawkins 7
63 Como-Pickton 0
50 Union Hill 0
73 Harmony 0
62 Leverett's Chapel 0
71 Mt Enterprise 0
91 Carlisle 0
65 Mildred 6
55 Axtell 0
48 Moody 0
28 Groom 2

824 Total (14 games) 15

Bloomington, CA (1994)

86 Big Bear 8
84 Notre Dame (Riv.) 0
62 West Valley 9
48 Valley View 14
72 Chaminade 14
40 Temescal Canyon 0
60 Rim of the World 28
60 Yucipa 12
68 La Sierra 27
66 Norte Vista 8
70 Sierra Vista 0
82 Artesia 62
34 Laguna Hills 21
48 La Mirada 32

880 Total (14 games) 235

INDEX

A

Aggressive blocking, 54, 57, 97
Angles, in 5-formation, 11
Attitude, of team members, 132
Awards, as motivation method, 140–41

B

Backside blocking, 21
Bag series drills, 173–74
Ball control, importance of, 184–85
Base blocking, and the toss, 20, 78
Bieniemy, Eric, 5
Black 24 toss, 66, 68, 77
Black 28 sweep, 71
Black 30 cut, 72
Blocking
   aggressive blocking, 54, 57
   backside blocking, 21
   base blocking, 20
   blocking scheme adjustments, 13–15
   down blocking, 14
   drive-till-you-die trap block, 35
   fill block, 59
   and 5-formation, 11
   half-man block, 20
   hook block, 62–63
   pivot block, 59
   P.P.blocking, 55
   seven technique, 22–23
   track blocking, 29
   wedge blocking, 47, 48
Bravo, Phil, 5, 87
Bulletin board, as motivation method, 140

C

Center, role of, 133–34
Chase drill, 180–81
Coaching error notes, post-game activities, 160
Combination drills, 171–72
Comeback, 116, 117
   I-left gold comeback, 117
Competition, encouragement of, 138–39
Cross toss
   aggressive blocking, 57
   backfield play, 41
   beginning play, 39–40
   failure, reasons for, 41
   4 S X-Toss Pass, 56–57
   guard actions, 43
   pre-snap, 42
   quarterback action, 42
   sustained fakes/sustained blocks, 43
   timing, importance of, 41
   24 X-toss, 40
   X-toss vs. even front, 40
   X-toss vs. odd front, 40

Cut (trap)
  beginning play, 33–34
  cut vs. even front, 35
  cut vs. odd front, 34
  cut option, 51
  downfield blocks set/runner up the seam, 38
  guard pulls/quarterback gives to fullback, 37
  pre-snap, 36
  stack-cut, 123
  wing fakes sweep/quarterback fakes bootleg, 37
  and wings-on, 71–72

D

Deception, and 5-formation, 12–13
Dive-cross-toss fake, 87
Dive
  30 Dive, 48
  wedge blocking, 47, 48
Dotson, David, 5
Double TE spread, 103
Down blocking, 14
Down and dirty drills, 174–75
Drag drill, 181
Dress practice, 149–50
Drills
  bag series drills, 173–74
  chase drill, 180–81
  combination drills, 171–72
  down and dirty drills, 174–75
  drag drill, 181
  fake drill, 178
  gauntlet drill, 180
  lane drill, 177
  live progression drills, 170
  log-block drills, 172–73
  offensive line agility drills, 165–66
  one-on-one drills, 175–76
  perfection drill, 185
  sled drills, 169–70
  sweep drill, 179
  timing drill, 178–79
  Z-series drills, 167–69
Drive-till-you-die trap block, 35

E

Explode, 59–60
  O Line P.P. block, 60
Explode-X, 60–61

F

Fade, 115–16
  I-left gold fade, 116
Fake drill, 178
Far boot, 62–63
  19 far naked bootleg, 63
Fill block, 59
5-formation, 7–14
  and blocking scheme adjustments, 13–15
  blocking schemes, 11
  cadence, nature of, 10
  and deception, 12–13
  and freeze sneak, 10
  fullback position, 8
  and keying tendencies, 9
  and no-play, 10
  performance, emphasis on, 10–11
  as team-offensive concept, 15
  tight splits, 8
  wing's motion route, 9
5-2 defense
  versus 24 reverse, 85
  versus 24 sweep, 122
  versus 24 toss, 73–74, 121
  versus 24 toss switch, 121
  versus 24 trap, 125
  versus 42 lead, 124
  versus 68 reverse, 126
  versus dive-cross-toss fake, 87
  versus guard trap, 90
  versus I-cut, 107
  versus I-left, 112
  versus I-sweep, 108
  versus I-trap, 109–10
  versus quarterback blast, 84

versus quarterback keep, 86
versus toss keep, 89
versus toss keep pass, 94
versus toss sweep, 87–88
versus wing to I toss, 92
versus yo-yo toss, 91
Flea-flicker, 57
Formation-play chart, 156
4 S X-Toss Pass, 56–57
Four-down concept, 186
Freeze sneak
   and 5-formation, 10
   and wedge blocking, 47, 48
Fullbacks, role of, 134

G

Game drive chart, 155
Game night, pre-game activities, 150–51
Gauntlet drill, 180
Green 24 toss, 66, 69–70, 79
Guards, role of, 133
Guard trap, 89–90
   versus 5-2 defense, 90

H

Half-man block, 20
Hitch, 118
   I-left gold hitch, 118
Hook block, 62–63

I

I-formation, 7, 99–103
   benefits of, 100–101
   comeback, 116, 117
   double TE I-formation, 100
   double TE spread, 103
   fade, 115–16
   hitch, 118
   I-cut, 106–7
   I-pitch pass, 113, 114–15
   I-scissors, 113, 114
   I-sweep, 108
   I-toss, 105–6
   I-trap, 109–10
   I-trap pass, 112–13
   I-twins formation, 102
   7 formation, 103
   slant, 116, 117
   stack-I formations, 102, 119–28
   unbalanced trips, 103
   as vertical offense, 100
Individual offense chart, 157

K

Kick-out blocks, 11
Knight, Ryan, 5

L

Lane drill, 177
Lead, stack-lead, 123
Live progression drills, 170
Log-block drills, 172–73
Lombardi, Vince, 27
Look-In pass, 54–56
   and open tight end, 56
   P.P.blocking, 55
   24 Look-In, 55

M

Markham, Don, 4, 73, 83, 85, 89, 101, 191
Motivation, 140–41
   recognition/rewards, 140–41

N

Naked Bootleg, 61–62
   near boot, 61–62
Namath, Joe, 183
Near Boot, 61–62
   19 near naked bootleg, 62
   19 far naked bootleg, 63
   19 near naked bootleg, 62

No-play, and 5-formation, 10
No-Play Pass, 48–49
   cadence in, 49

O

Offensive line agility drills, 165–66
O Line aggressive blocks, 54
O Line P.P. block, 60
One-on-one drills, 175–76
Outflanking, example of, 88

P

Passing, running versus, 188–90
Pettingill, Mark, 6
Philosophy of team, 190
Pitch pass, 63–64
   I-pitch pass, 113, 114
   play action in, 64
   and toss action, 63–64
Pivot block, 59
Play selection, elements of, 186
the play
   meaning of, 19
   See also specific plays by name
Post-game activities
   coaching error notes, 160
   formation/play adjustments, 162
   formation-play chart, 156
   game drive chart, 155
   individual drill chart by position, 163
   individual mistake chart, 158
   individual offense chart, 157
   personnel adjustment, 161
   praise charts, 159
P.P. blocking, 55, 60
Practice schemes
   defense, 148–49
   dress practice, 149–50
   offense, 147–48
   review/preparation/light practice, 146
   team sled work, 146–47
   video screening of opponent, 146–47, 148
Praise charts, 159

Q

Quarterback, role of, 134–36
Quarterback blast, 83–84
   10 blast, 83, 84
Quarterback keep, 86
   versus 5-2 defense, 86

R

Reverse, 85, 98
   versus 5-2 defense, 85
   24 reverse, 85–86, 98
Royster, Mazio, 5
Running, versus passing, 188–90
Running trick plays, 187
Russell, Leonard, 5

S

Scissors pass, 57–59, 95–96
   blocking in, 59
   deep pass, 96
   18 scissors pass, 58, 95
   I-scissors pass, 113, 114
   QB throwback, 96
   setting up pass, 58
Scoring
   double point values, 188
   and time factor, 188
7-formation, 103
7-technique, 14, 69
   and the toss, 22–23
   and 24 toss, 78
7-1 defense, versus 24 toss, 76–77
7-2 defense, versus 24 toss, 74–75
6-5 defense, versus 24 toss, 77–79
6-2 defense
   versus quarterback blast, 84
   versus 24 toss, 76
60 Cut, 50
Size, of team members, 132

Slant, 116
  I-left gold slant, 117
Sled drills, 169–70
Sneak
  QB sneak on sound, 48
  wedge blocking, 47, 48
Speed, of team members, 132
Speed pass, 97
Stack-I formations, 102, 119–28
  stack-cut, 123
  stack-lead, 123, 124
  stack-sweep, 122–23
  stack-switch, 120, 121
  stack-tight end reverse, 126
  stack-toss, 120
  stack-trap, 125
  stack-trap pass, 127–28
Stack-I set, 7
Strength, of team members, 132
Sweep drill, 179
Sweep
  beginning play, 27–28
  defense stuck inside/guard leads runner around end, 32
  defensive end, attack of, 29–30
  fate to fullback/guards pull, 31
  pre-snap, 31
  stack-sweep, 122–23
  sweep vs. even front, 29
  sweep vs. odd front, 28
  and track blocking, 29
  wing cracks back/gives to wing-back, 31
  and Wing-T play, 30

T

Tackles, role of, 133
Team
  center, 133–34
  fullbacks, 134
  guards, 133
  philosophy of, 190
  player qualities for, 132
  quarterback, 134–36
  tackles, 133
  tight ends, 133
  wings, 134
10 blast, 83, 84
30 Dive, 48
Tight End counters, 60 Cut, 50
Tight end reverse, stack-tight end reverse, 126
Tight ends, role of, 133
Tight splits, 8
Timing drill, 178–79
Toss, 53–54
  backside blocking, 21
  backside pulling, 25
  base blocking vs. ODD front, 20
  base technique, 19
  basis of success of, 19
  history of, 3–5
  O Line aggressive blocks, 54
  pitch, 26
  pre-snap, 25
  runner into seam, 26
  running to sideline, 187–88
  and seven technique, 22–23
  toss keep/toss option, 49–51
  and tunnel technique, 23–24
  and window technique, 24
  wings, moving on first hit, 21–22
  wing's running lane, 22
  working the play, 186–87
Toss keep pass, 93–94
  versus 5-2 defense, 89, 94
Toss sweep, 87–88
  versus 5-2 defense, 88
Track blocking, 29
Training
  competition, encouragement of, 138–39
  football drills, 138
  games, 138
  motivation, 140–41
  weightlifting, 137–38
Trap
  stack-trap, 125
  stack-trap pass, 127–28
  trap blocks, 11
  See also Cut (trap)